The
Hotel Tacloban

The
Hotel Tacloban

Douglas Valentine

AN AUTHORS GUILD BACKINPRINT.COM EDITION

AN AUTHORS GUILD BACKINPRINT.COM EDITION

Published by iUniverse.com, Inc.

For information address:
iUniverse.com, Inc.
620 North 48th Street, Suite 201
Lincoln, NE 68504-3467
www.iuniverse.com

Originally published by Lawrence Hill & Co., Inc.

ISBN: 0-595-00785-6

Printed in the United States of America

to Alice
to Chris
and
to Dad

Author's Note

As is probably the case with most boys born during the post-war baby boom, I was fascinated by the glorified accounts of World War Two I watched regularly on television and at the movies: John Wayne fighting to the finish on Bataan; Vic Morrow and his scruffy buddies rolling across France in "Combat"; Robert Mitchum, Van Johnson, William Bendix and a battalion of Hollywood's bravest leading men making the world safe for freedom and democracy. I must admit, as a little kid I was very impressed. My friends and I thought that nothing could be finer than to follow in the foxholes of our fathers. We asked for, and got, toy guns at Christmas, with which we fought make-believe battles in the hardwood forests behind our Westchester homes. The Japs were everywhere and you had to be careful not to expose yourself unnecessarily.

"Bang! Got ya!"

"No you didn't! I got *you* first!" Etc.

Some of us playing soldier, myself included, were lucky enough to have a father who had actually been there (if you did, you might even have in your possession an authentic US Army helmet, or a genuine Japanese bayonet with inscriptions), and I, for one, was always pestering mine to tell me exactly what he did in the war. "Did you shoot any Japs? Huh, Dad?" He chuckled, rubbed my head, and satisfied my curiosity with a slew of bizarre anecdotes, all of which, cross my heart, were absolutely true.

Like the time he saw a tank roll over an unsuspecting GI on a beach at Fort Ord, California, just before he was shipped overseas. The incident occurred during a mock amphibious landing being staged for some visiting brass. It was early morning, low tide. A line of infantrymen was spread out along the shoreline while behind them an armored company was disembarking from LSTs. The site itself had been chosen specifically because the sand there was unusually loose and granular and would demonstrate just how effectively the DUKWs and other assorted amphibious vehicles were at maneuvering over difficult terrain—the type the US Army was expecting to encounter in the South Pacific. Anyway, in the noise and confusion, one tank accidentally veered off course and in a split second, before anyone had a chance to react, it had rolled over some poor son-of-a-bitch who was napping when he should have been wide awake. What happened next, however, is the truly amazing part: the soldier popped-up uninjured to a chorus of cheers and a standing ovation from his slap-happy comrades. The tank had merely pressed him into the sand. According to my father, it was the sort of extraordinary experience that left a lasting impression on anyone who'd witnessed it.

Then there was the time, several months later and halfway around the world, when he saw a spent bullet enter a soldier's helmet about an inch above the guy's left ear, spin around the back, exit about an inch above the right ear and spit out onto the ground. The startled GI removed his helmet to see what damage had been done, and when he did, his hair came off with it. He'd been scalped!

Dear old Dad had an endless supply of war stories like those two, most of which centered on jokes played on inept second lieutenants by mischievous enlisted men. Nevertheless, as I grew older and began asking harder questions, like, "Whatever became of the fellows standing next to you in the pictures in the family photo album?" Dad suddenly became defensive, or got annoyed, or brushed me aside with the same old excuse that, "Soldiers don't like to talk about those things." I sensed that he was holding something back, something significant, and wanting to get at the truth, I persisted. But my father's will was stronger than mine. As the years went by, he steadfastly refused to break his vow of silence, and eventually I just stopped asking why.

My father was not like other veterans I knew. He did keep some treasured, faded photographs of friends in uniform, but he wouldn't march in the Memorial Day parade, nor would he allow real guns in the house, nor would he have anything to do with the US Army or with veterans organizations like the VFW or the American Legion. He didn't like the way those people went around patting each other on the back and bragging about battles they'd never fought. Most of them, he insisted, weren't combat soldiers anyway, because the majority of front line soldiers were still there, right where they'd fallen.

When it came to explaining my father's reclusive behavior, or why he held a grudge against the US Army, my mother wasn't much help, either; I got the feeling that she'd been sworn to secrecy, *if* she knew anything at all. She was forever pleading with Dad to seek financial aid from the VA for the multiple medical problems he'd incurred during the war (he had terrible malaria attacks which laid him up for a few days every spring and fall, and his front teeth were missing, and there were other things wrong, too—things I didn't know about at the time), but he wouldn't hear of it. He avoided the Army like the plague. And rather than stooping to ask it for help, financial or otherwise, he buried himself in two jobs; he worked days driving a truck for Railway Express out of Mount Kisco, and he worked six nights a week part-time at the King's Crown liquor store in Pleasantville. Not just for the money. It was like he was running away from something horrible. Like he was trying to hide from his past.

For a long time I had the feeling that my father was avoiding me, and as I grew older, through junior high and high school— through the first years of the Vietnam War—he and I grew progressively further apart. We disagreed on just about everything, including Vietnam, and when it came time for me to head off to college, I couldn't get away from home fast enough. Meanwhile, Dad continued to grind himself into the ground, the war dragged on, and I acquired a small amount of knowledge sufficient to do myself harm. I dropped out of school in my senior year, came home to collect my belongings and, during a heated argument that ensued, accused my father of harboring a death wish. How I came up with a statement like that I'll never know, but two months later, as if to prove me right, on spite, he had his first massive heart attack. I hit the road for California a few weeks after that.

Dad lived on borrowed time for the next ten years, never knowing when or if the time-bomb in his chest was going to explode. During those ten years, I'm sad to say, we had very little to do with one another; in fact, it wasn't until two years ago, on his doctor's advice, that we finally sat down together to patch up our differences. And that's when I learned what really happened in the war. For the first time I heard about the nightmares, visions and flashbacks that had driven him to the brink of madness for so many years.

Not only did I learn why my father loathed the Army, but I learned about his childhood, too. It was not a happy time. His mother, Gladys Jensen, and his father, Garnet Day Spence (a rogue who couldn't hold down a job) divorced before he was one, and he was sent to live with one relative after another until, four years later, his mother re-married and took him home. A fractious child with curly blond hair and hazel eyes, he was prone to throwing wild temper tantrums for no apparent reason; he spent two years of his life—ages nine and ten—bedridden with polio; and throughout his youth he played second fiddle to a favored older brother, as well as to his younger step-brother and step-sister. I learned that his boyhood idols were Alvin Cullum York and Sid Luckman; that his ambition was to enroll in a military academy like West Point; and that he was Pleasantville's first Eagle Scout. My father's favorite sport was boxing and he was very good with his fists. He ran away from home when he was fourteen and wound up in Albany washing dishes in a series of downtown kitchens, and he lied about his age and enlisted in the Army when he was sixteen. I learned that he met Bobby Stevenson in the Army, that they became best friends (Bobby understood that there was something missing from my father's life), and that Bobby died in his arms in New Guinea. And I learned about the Hotel Tacloban.

I learned how, at the age of fifty-six, the faces which had haunted him day and night, for almost forty years, finally became too much for him to bear. I learned how my father sought psychiatric help after his second open-heart surgery, and how the doctor convinced him to tell the truth about what happened in the war, even though, by doing so, he risked arousing the wrath of the US Army. Never one to worry too much about risk, Dad took his doctor's advice and told me the whole unbelievable story, which I recorded on tape then copied down on the following pages.

Before you dig in, I'd like to mention something revealing my father said to me on the day John Kennedy was assassinated. I'll never forget that day—it was the day of his mother's funeral. I'd heard the news of Kennedy's death on the TV and I'd gone into the living room, where the adults were consoling one another, to let everyone know. I was fourteen at the time and the first person I told was my grandfather, who didn't hear a word I said, and who, when I repeated myself, pulled away from me and sobbed, "I don't care." Next I told my father the awful news. "Dad," I said excitedly, "the President's been shot and they got the guy who did it." More kindly than bitterly, he replied, "The guy they got didn't do it, Doug. You can count on that."

That really set me back on my heels. Like I said, I was only 14 then—just a kid—and it frightened me to think that there was something sinister—something deadly—about my Dad. After hearing what happened to him in the war and at the Hotel Tacloban, you too will understand exactly why that is.

Foreword

Right after my first heart attack, while I was flat on my back on the operating table in the emergency ward, and the doctors were hooking me up to the jumper cables and the nurses were wondering out loud what my religion was. ("If he's a Catholic, they'd better get a priest in here quick," one of them said.) I was wracked by feelings of profound anguish, not from any fear of death, but anguish arising from an overriding concern for the fate of my family, should I die. "My God," I thought. "What's going to happen to Kitty and the kids if I don't pull through this thing? How are they going to make it from now on without me? We finally moved into a place that's halfway decent, and now they'll have to leave. My God! What have I done?"

I felt, rightfully so, that I'd failed them, and I felt terrible guilt for having allowed the heart attack to occur. For weeks I'd been having shortness of breath and palpitations, and I knew perfectly well that it was coming on, but something deep inside me—a feeling that I had no right to be alive—prevented me from going to the doctor. Another guilt from another time, long ago; guilt which had hounded me day and night for thirty years in nightmares, visions and flashbacks; survivor's guilt from World War Two, rising in my subconscious mind, like a ghost from the grave, to claim its due.

But I survived that heart attack, and another one, and open-heart surgery twice, and seven strokes, and I realized, with the help of family, doctors and friends, that *somehow*, if I ever hoped to find peace of mind, I had to exorcise from my soul the survivor's guilt which had tormented me for so many years. So it was that I came to dictate this book.

For all of my adult life I tried to justify the things I did and the things which were done to me, in the war and in the Hotel Tacloban, by telling myself that it was a question of self-preservation, or that I was trapped by circumstances beyond my control, or that I was a victim, perhaps, of culture. Not anymore. I know now that it's not up to me to say *who* or *what* was to blame. Telling what happened is, and that I've done. And let me assure you that I've gained an abiding sense of satisfaction from having done my part to set the record straight. Lord knows the authorities haven't put forth an explanation.

Doug Valentine
April 13, 1983
Briarcliff Manor

"Taubada, when I write, it is too hard to write the truth. To write the words is hard, but I could never write all the words to tell all the truth. To write at all I must make all the things seem easy. Then, when it is written, it is not all the truth. Some of the words are not the right words, because I am tired with writing. Do you think the men who write history are like that? Are you like that when you write, taubada?"

Gibson Duluvina, a Papuan, speaking to his taubada (master) Osmar White, an Australian war correspondent in New Guinea in 1942. Papuans have no written history. The quote above is from White's *Green Armor* (W. W. Norton and Company, Inc, New York, 1944; pages 152-153).

The
Hotel Tacloban

Chapter One

New Guinea. The first time I heard of it, I was on a troopship three weeks into the Pacific Ocean. I didn't know where it was, or what it was, or anything else about it, and neither did anyone else.

We had just crossed the equator when the announcement came over the PA system informing us that our destination was New Guinea, second largest island in the world after Greenland, as they so blandly described it. What they neglected to say, however, was that it was an abomination; a rotten stinking hellhole of incessant rains and horrendous temperatures consistently pushing 120 degrees; a pressure cooker where everything lived and died at an accelerated rate of speed; a Stone Age world populated by cannibals armed with blowguns and poison darts; a nightmare land of six inch spiders, fifteen pound rats, and unimaginable disease.

New Guinea. It even looked evil on the map circulating from hold to hold, like a gigantic dragon flying west in between northern Australia and the equator. The dragon's enormous jaws (seen on the map as MacCleur Gulf) appeared wide open, as if the beast were preparing to swallow whole the numerous Molucca Islands of Indonesia. And protruding from the dragon's jagged spine, the Owen Stanley Mountain Range formed a lethal, razorbacked tail extending into the Coral Sea. Those treacherous hills would be the scene of our first combat with elements of Japan's elite corps of jungle fighters, the vaunted South Seas Detachment.

Beginning in late July, 1942, the first of about 10,000 of those veteran troops were put ashore halfway down the the dragon's tail at the tiny coastal village of Buna. Setting out in a southwesterly direction, the Japanese vanguard immediately began its trek across the gruelling Kokoda Trail, an endeavor considered *impossible* by the Allied military braintrust in Brisbane, Australia. On the other side of the Owen

Stanleys, 100 miles away topographically but ten times as far in reality, sat Tokyo's primary objective in the South Pacific— Port Moresby.

Why ransacked, rundown Port Moresby? Because Moresby had an excellent deep-water harbor capable of accomodating an entire convoy, plus which it was ringed by seven airdromes Tokyo had every intention of using as launching pads for its planned invasion of Australia. The Aussies, who governed Northeast New Guinea and the Territory of Papua and who were legally responsible for administering the campaign, were aware of this of course, but their professional soldiers were all off in North Africa, the Mideast or Malaya, fighting, as usual, England's war. They had been recalled, but they had yet to arrive, and by early August the veteran Japanese had fought their way up the north face of the Owen Stanleys to Kokoda Village; they were halfway to Moresby and meeting only minimal resistance from an out-numbered and ill-equipped Australian force composed of Home Guard militiamen.

That's when we appeared on the scene. Ours was a provisional unit (a hastily assembled cadre of combat-engineers organized by the discombobulated Army Ground Forces and assigned to the 32nd Division) which was heading to Australia to hook-up with the 32nd for further training in amphibious operations (our basic training so far had consisted of two passes through the gashouse—once with a mask, once without—48 hours in a bivouac area, and five shots on the rifle range) when it was unexpectedly diverted to New Guinea to serve as a temporary plug in the faltering Australian lines. Basically, we were a good-will gesture from General Douglas MacArthur to the beleagured Aussies, who had been perfectly willing to give that worthless piece of real estate to the Japanese for free—until MacArthur in his wisdom persuaded them to do otherwise.

He would be delighted to help them, sure, but only on the condition that our presence in New Guinea remained top secret. To protect himself just in case the Owen Stanley Campaign turned into another catastrophe like the one at Bataan, Dougout Doug, when issuing official communiques, made no mention of the fact that American ground forces were fighting and dying in New Guinea. Things would change dramatically once the Japanese tide had been turned, but until then his lips were sealed.

Of course, I shouldn't place *all* the blame on General MacArthur; censorship is an absolute must at the start of any war, if only to ensure that the necessary flow of volunteers back home continues uninterrupted.

In accordance with its designation as combat-engineer, my unit was divided into two more or less equal parts, the first half consisting of a boat battalion (Higgins boat operators and such) for transporting combat elements from ship to shore during amphibious operations. The second half was composed of a shore battalion with its GHQ situated on the beach (where our commanders could congregate in comparative safety and comfort), one near-shore company for handling supplies and equipment on the beach (as well as for maintaining a lucrative black market), and four far-shore companies (mine being one of these) for defending said beach. Immediately upon our arrival in Paleolithic New Guinea, those of us in the far-shore companies hiked 25 murderous miles inland to form a defensive perimeter on Imita Ridge, in the vicinity of the Goldie River. A combined company command post, consisting of a table in a tent for our officers to eat at while they discussed strategy and commiserated with one another, was established. The enlisted men pitched their two-man pup tents in a circle around the officers' tent and took turns on sentry duty. There were reports of scattered Japanese patrols in the area and everyone was very uptight.

Our immediate orders were to stop the Japanese from slipping into Moresby through the jungles west of Imita Ridge, and, if the need should arise, to participate in amphibious landings up and down the coast. The situation was this: the Japanese 144th Regiment was cascading over the Owen Stanleys and fanning out to our north and west. In most places they were swarming over the badly outnumbered Aussies sent to stop them. Where we were, they were already within thirty miles of their objective. By fighting in the aggressive style for

5

which they are world famous, by plunging into the forest and outflanking the Aussies, who stuck to the trails, the Japanese had succeeded in pushing the 39th and 53rd Battalions (Australian Home Guard) out of Ioribaiwa Village and they were massing there, less than five miles from our perimeter.

For the next month we were locked in a stalemate with the Japanese. From our position on the crest of Imita Ridge we watched in the panoramic distance as Japanese light bombers, which we called Charleys, dropped food and equipment to their forward supply dump at Nauro Creek—about five miles behind Ioribaiwa. While our Fifth Air Force B-17 and A-20 bombers hammered Nauro Creek, our heavy artillery (105mm and 155mm howitzers, and 25 pounders) kept up a protracted bombardment of the Japanese infantry entrenchments across the Ua-ale Valley. At the same time our own transport planes were zooming in over base camp at tree top level, kicking out bundles of supplies and equipment, half of which were irretrivably lost in the inpenetrable jungle maze. Native carriers from Moresby (some dressed only in leaves, some stark naked, some with thin slivers of bone shoved through their nostrils, others with dried blood smeared on their ebony chests) continued to carry up more and more cases of ammunition and medicine, and there was an inordinate flurry of activity around forward HDQs, all of which prompted our old-time sergeants to speculate that an offensive move was in the offing. As usual, they were right.

Then a week passed in mid-September in which there was very little contact with forward Japanese patrols, as well as diminishing traces of their main force (once numbering about 5,000 men) at Ioribaiwa. These were precisely the signs our commanders had been looking for and, consequently, they decided that the time was right to launch an offensive of their own. According to Intelligence reports gleaned from aerial photography (useless in the jungle) and native reports (notoriously unreliable), the South Seas Detachment had, in its haste to reach and conquer Moresby, badly overextended itself and was now completely cut-off from supply and communication lines. We were told that New Guinea was working its wicked magic on our enemy—that sick and starving Japanese soldiers were scrounging through the jungle, and that the little bastards were finished as a fighting force.

What we weren't told, and what our Intelligence officers didn't know, was that Tokyo had ordered the South Seas Detachment to withdraw back to Buna for transfer to Guadalcanal, where US Marines were slowly but surely winning the battle for that strategically more important island. In any event, the veteran Australian 7th Division, looking rakish in slouch hats and shorts, had finally arrived from Libya, plus which the 32nd Division had arrived from Brisbane and was waiting in the wings. Thus, sometime in late September, we began our own trek over the monstrous Owen Stanleys. Incidentally, our forward move marked an historically significant turning point in World War Two; from the morning of our advance, right up to VJ-day, the Japanese would steadily lose ground, straight back to mainland Japan and defeat. They would never get any closer to Australia than Ioribaiwa.

When the South Seas Department realized they'd been abandoned by their high command, they cut their losses and retreated northeast, back the way they'd come two months before. In the wake of their retreat my unit forged ahead, systematically gaining ground measured in yards, digging in, calling up mortar crews, artillery and air power to blast into smithereens whatever opposition lay ahead. Spearheading the assault was the infantry, our depleted companies continually reforming and consolidating until, after two weeks of uninterrupted advancing, the four original companies had been reduced to two. Replacements never materialized and those of us who remained began to think and act like professional soldiers. The gradual disintegration of our unit, coupled with the loss of our comrades and the insanity of our surroundings, had a profound numbing effect on each and every one of us. The change had occurred a fraction at a time, without our knowing it, but we could now face the most horrible and bizarre sights without batting an eye.

We didn't know what to expect anymore. There was no semblance of order, only a sense of flux. In the course of a "normal" day we encountered groups of men sitting around in mournful silence, or we were passed by groups of men hustling frantically from one place to another. We saw men wandering aimlessly in a trance, mute, unable to mutter above a whisper, or men so badly shell-shocked that their hands had to be pried from their rifles. Men simply disappeared. And what with Japanese snipers penetrating within our perimeter, either sneaking in under cover of darkness or hiding underground or up in trees as we moved ever-onward, death could surface anytime, anywhere. There was so much madness going on, such a feeling of distance from everyone and everything, that we stopped making judgements about anyone's behavior. Surviving became our one and only concern.

During this numbing period on the line I experienced my first malaria attack. I was sitting in my foxhole feeling flushed, and sweat was pouring out of me, but I ignored those early warning signs, attributing them to the constant physical exertion, to the extreme heat and humidity. Before too long, however, I was having icy chills, dizzyness and shakes, then the trees began to spin and the shrubs began to dance around me and I was gone. I became so useless to my comrades that they called for the medics and had me carried to a field hospital tent in a rear area where I ranted and raved deliriously for the next three days.

At the time I contracted malaria, I was totally unaware of the ramifications, although it would prove to be the bane of my existence for the next few years. I had no idea that cerebral malaria—which is found only in the fetid lowland swamps of New Guinea—kills one third of its victims outright and wreaks ungodly havoc on the minds and bodies of the others. Desensitized by my insane surroundings, I couldn't admit to myself that I had a disease, or that it could do me harm. The medics warned me to wait, to give things a chance to calm down, but my mental processes had been derailed by the disease and to my distorted way of thinking, malaria in itself was not a valid reason for abandoning my friends.

I know that sounds ridiculous, but no one set me straight. The Army was unwilling to admit that malaria, which was putting over fifty percent of our men out of action, was a serious problem; because it was a disease, not a combat wound, and because it required the services of able-bodied soldiers who might otherwise be on the line, any man down with malaria was treated like an unnecessary burden. There was a terrible stigma attached to it, almost as if anyone who had contracted it was malingering. Between the adverse mental effects of the disease, and the negative way it was viewed, I just did not know what to do. So the moment the fever and chills subsided, I returned to the line and took up my position beside my comrades.

Once I started having malaria attacks—attacks which occurred regularly every few weeks—I was never again as strong as I had been before. Devoid of stamina, I found it increasingly hard to function, mentally as well as physically. One part of me wanted very much to call it quits, to spare myself the pain and misery, and my friends urged me to have myself shipped back to an area where I could receive adequate medical attention, but I refused. After all that we had been through together, I just couldn't leave them alone. Meanwhile our unit moved relentlessly ahead, chasing the Japanese further and further into the hills, and with each passing day I grew more and more exhausted. I kept praying that we'd stop, or get relieved, but more than anything else I wished that the goddamned war would go away.

The US Army had other plans. Once the momentum had swung in our favor, we were little more than flotsam swept along on the tide of the forward movement. All of our time was spent tramping through the twilight gloom of bamboo forests, or through mangrove swamps thick with wide buttressed banyan trees, or across sun-drenched fields of kunai grass. We skirted pools of deadly quicksand and we trudged through the stinking, greyish-brown peat bogs which were a common feature of the water-logged terrain. Some were as large as football fields, some were the size of swimming pools, all had rotten logs and decaying branches jutting out of their foul, porridge-like mass. Swarms of mosquitoes floated above the algae-covered surface, but we walked right through. The silt seeped into our pants and boots, making us feel like we were being dragged under by the weight, and the slimy layer of mud on the bottom made it hard to keep your footing, but we kept right on going.

We crossed frothing streams on slippery, moss-coated logs and we tramped endlessly through ankle-deep mud. Mud. Mud. Mud. Huge black clouds engulfed the towering mountain tops; awesome thunderstorms shook the earth and we were drenched in endless torrential rains. Yet nowhere in that stinking swamp was fresh water to be found—native carriers had to lug our precious, purified drinking water from base camps on the beach. There was never any place to bathe, never an opportunity to engage in the luxury of personal hygene, and under such conditions it became impossible to properly care for ourselves. All manner of odious vermin were constantly preying on our bodies, causing us profound discomfort. Our skin was covered with jungle rot, bloodsucking leeches, and infected insect bites. We never had a change of clothes; we had one pair of pants, one shirt, and one tattered poncho which we tore into long strips and wrapped around our rifles in an effort to keep them dry. It didn't help, but we did it anyway.

Thirsty and sweaty, filthy and soaking wet, sick to our stomachs from dysentery and burning up with fever, we pushed through the lush Ua-ale Valley to the steep green cliffs and rocky precipices that signalled the start of the Owen Stanleys. Clinging to heaving, bucking paths where no jeep could even dream of going—some pitched at violent 60 degree angles— we said goodbye to the foothills and clawed our way into the mountains.

Chapter Two

Approximately two weeks into the advance a number of men in my outfit were pulled off the line and sent down to Moresby to participate in a small amphibious landing. GHQ was having a problem with Japanese troops approaching Moresby in square-nosed barges, and even though the air force was raising hell with them, there was evidence of coastal infiltration. GHQ's response was to have the navy transport a contingent of Australian and American infantrymen up the coast to directly assault these new Japanese positions.

Despite the dangers of an amphibious operation, none of us were overly concerned; we were certain that it could not be any worse than what we had been enduring on the line. We also knew that we would have a few days of rest and relaxation before the operation, so those were the best orders we had received in a long time.

As expected, we were given a few days to ourselves when we arrived in Moresby, time we devoted to laying around doing nothing but eating warm meals, sleeping in tents out of the rain, playing cards, or standing for hours under homemade showers consisting of a row of buckets, each one having several holes punched in its bottom and a hose strapped over its top. We made the most of our brief vacation from the tensions of the line, except for one thing. There had been four of us in the beginning, starting with basic training at Camp Knight, then coming across on the troopship. Now there were three. There was me, Doug Valentine, sixteen, not too bright, runaway from a broken home in Pleasantville, New York, an orphan of the Great Depression. There was my best friend, Bobby Stevenson, eighteen, deeply religious farm boy and high school basketball player from Elkheart County, Indiana. And there was Charley Ferguson, twenty-five, married, previously employed in the General Motors plant in St Louis, Missouri. The fourth member of our little group, Andor "Andy" Landeren, a stout Norwegian merchant seaman who had been stranded on the high seas when Germany invaded Norway in the spring of 1940, had been killed during the first day of the forward move.

Andy had stepped on a land mine and, from what the guys who had been there said, he had died instantly. We all felt terribly bad about that, but what made it worse was that neither Bobby nor Charley nor I had been with him when it happened. We felt that we had let him down. And now that we were safe and idle, we found it harder than ever to accept the fact that Andy was dead. Andy had been one of us and now that he was gone, a piece of each of us was lost forever too. But we tried our best not to dwell on the subject; instead, we lost ourselves in the utter chaos that was Port Moresby. We did what soldiers do. We took it a day at a time.

On the day prior to the landing operation, GHQ assembled about 600 Australian and American infantrymen on one of Port Moresby's newly constructed docks, loaded us into a flotilla of smaller craft, and ferried us out to three larger vessels sitting in the hazy harbor. It was a nice day in New Guinea; it was hot and humid, of course, but it wasn't raining. When we got aboard, everyone was quartered on the top decks, which was unusual and may have been the result of the favorable weather conditions.

This was going to be the first joint landing operation of the campaign and the brass were excited and enthusiastic. We weren't. But I did feel pretty good about being out on the water, away from the grime and the bugs and the claustrophobia of the jungle, and my spirits were up—comparatively speaking. Each of us, however, has his private phobias, and Bobby's just happened to be water. He confided to me that he had never learned how to swim, and he said that he was uncomfortable about going into the operation, maybe even a little bit scared.

That didn't seem right. Bobby was my rock of Gibraltar; the one person I could trust to be there when I needed him. Like on the first day of the forward move, when we met such fierce resistance. A mortar shell had landed near us and a boy was lying in the underbrush holding his stomach and crying; a fragment from the shell had ripped his belly wide open and I could see his hands groping blindly in the wound, as if he were trying to stem the flow of blood with his fingers. Another boy was lying on his back on a splintered tree stump with his guts trailing out of his abdomen, hideously, like a human sacrifice spread out on some pagan altar. Just by looking at him I knew he was dead. The other boy with the gaping stomach wound was crying out for his mother and one of the Japanese up ahead was jeering at him, saying, "Go ahead and cly, Yankee! Soon enough you all be dead!" At that moment I just wanted to throw down my gun and get the hell out of there. Let them do whatever they wanted to me, I just didn't care.

Then I turned to Bobby, who was in a kneeling position, squeezing off shots at the place where he thought the voice had originated. As usual he was a rock, calm and precise, and in the midst of all that confusion he paused for a moment, looked at me reassuringly and said, "Come on, Doug. We gotta do *something* or we'll go crazy." He smiled, and suddenly the feeling of panic turned into a feeling that bordered on rage. Suddenly I was more concerned about Bobby than I was about myself. Something clicked into place. I felt transformed. Knowing that I had to do my share, I picked up my rifle, knelt beside Bobby, and started shooting.

Until he had enlisted in the Army at the age of eighteen, Bobby Stevenson had never been more than fifty or sixty miles away from the good-sized farm in Indiana where he was born and raised, and yet he was as mature and self-reliant as someone ten years older and ten times as well traveled. Bobby had clean-cut good looks, dark wavy hair, dark brown eyes, a square jaw and loose, long limbs. He was four inches taller than me and he outweighed me by thirty-five pounds, all of it the kind of lean hard muscle that comes from routine farm work and sports. He was fast on his feet, poised, and exceptionally graceful for a farm boy. But above all, Bobby was a magnificent soldier; not only was he a crack shot and all-around firearms expert, but he was the enlisted man most trusted by our company sergeant and surrogate father, Harry

Blackman. Out of all of us, Bobby had the best attitude, too. It was he who said, and made us realize, that the sooner we took the offensive and cleaned the little bastards out of that hellhole they called New Guinea, the sooner we could all go home.

That's why I was so concerned. I'd never seen Bobby get uptight about anything before, and I desperately wanted to relieve his anxiety (fear is contagious), so I scouted around the ship until I located an agreeable sailor who knew where the life jackets were stowed and was willing to borrow one for me. The life jacket itself was a real oldtimer, made out of square blocks of cork strung together, lacking a collar. It fit like a bulky vest, and it looked ridiculous, and Charley started teasing Bobby the moment he tried it on for size, but it was better than nothing and it made Bobby feel more confident.

We put out of Moresby about noon, a few tired looking destroyers hooking up with us once we were out beyond the harbor, then we started chugging along the coast, close enough to shore to see the palm trees swaying. That night we sprawled on deck beneath the bright tropical moon, rocking on the waves and marvelling at the brilliant Southern Cross, which beamed overhead like a silent benediction. Bobby and Charley were stretched out on either side of me, and nearby a group of Aussies was singing:

> *Bless 'em all. Bless 'em all.*
> *The long and the short and the tall.*
> *Bless all the sergeants and all of their guns,*
> *Bless all the corporals and their blinking sons.*
> *Cause we're saying goodbye to them all,*
> *As back to their foxholes they crawl.*
> *You'll get no promotion this side of the ocean,*
> *So cheer up my lads, bless 'em all.*

The ships never hove-to that night, but proceeded at a snail's pace until morning, with those of us who could catching a few hours shuteye on the crowded, squirming deck.

With the sunrise came the thunderous roar of naval gunfire and the banshee wail of Air Force bombers making their runs on the beachhead. The air was filled with smoke, the jungle fringe was a sheet of flame; on the beach itself, columns of sand and debris mushroomed into the sky, almost scraping the bottoms of the planes swooping in low. It was an awesome sight, one which filled us with a sense of power. After each barrage, the destroyers firing at the Japanese positions were actually pushed back in the water by the recoil from their cannons. Empty landing craft were orbiting around the larger ships like planets in adjacent solar systems, then falling out of orbit, one by one, and pulling alongside the cargo nets hanging down from the troop carriers. Bobby and I were in the first group of soldiers that climbed down the cargo nets into the Higgins boats. Charley was in the second. We shoved off and started to circle while the other boats were being filled.

The Higgins boats were 36 feet long and held about two dozen tightly packed men. They used standard Detroit diesel engines, had flat bottoms that enabled them to drive up onto the beach, and they had square prows which flopped down to form unloading ramps. They were a big improvement from what we were used to. Until they had been introduced, most of our amphibious landings had been unmitigated disasters. Nevertheless, the Higgins boats had their weaknesses. Because they were fabricated out of a lightweight material resembling plywood, and because they had flat bottoms, they bobbed around a lot on the ocean, so that, after fifteen minutes, anyone who was prone to seasickness became violently ill. Indeed, assaulting a beachhead is the type of experience that tends to turn a man's stomach anyway, and half the men in our boat were doubled over, retching, while the other half knelt, prayed, and held their breath.

Bobby and I had become separated when we entered the craft and from where I stood, in the stern, I could see him crouching in the bow, holding his hand to his mouth. I knew he was sick, and that worried me. But we had to wait for over an hour, until all the landing craft were loaded and lined up and ready to hit the beach, and by the time we finally did start in, I was no longer certain where we were in relation to the other boats, or how far we had to go, because the armored bowplate obstructed my view. Curious to know, I stuck my head above the gunnel to get a better look; we were approximately 500 yards from shore and there was nothing for me to see except sea and sky and Higgins boats following behind us. Only the coxswain had a clear view from his station in the elevated stern. As we plunged through a gap in the reef, he signalled for us to get ready and I dropped down inside. The roar of the naval and air force barrage combined with the reverbarating diesel engines to drown out all other sounds within the hollow craft; it was impossible to hear the man beside you, and it was useless to try to move, so Bobby and I remained apart. However, the deafening noise of our guns and planes seemed to be insulating us from harm, and I thought we'd be okay for the time being.

For the next ten minutes we took no fire from the Japanese positions. We were within two hundred yards of the beach, and had just finished preparing ourselves to disembark, when our own guns fell silent and the Japanese opened up. Almost immediately there was a terrific explosion; first I felt the wave of heat, even before I heard the shell explode, then I felt myself being flung out of the boat, into the sea. We had taken a direct hit.

The next thing I remember, I was sinking beneath the water, struggling to remove my helmet and the heavy gear strapped on my back, then becoming buoyant and rising to the surface. Before I could gulp air, I first had to spit out a belly-full of warm salty sea water mixed with blood. My ears ringing, my head throbbing, I instinctively began to tread water. When I finally got my head screwed on right I immediately looked around for Bobby but he was nowhere in sight, so I began to swim in ever-widening circles, searching for him amongst the pieces of wreckage and equipment and bodies strewn about. There was a great deal of panic and confusion in the water; badly wounded men were thrashing and screaming hysterically and reaching out for help. The sea was churning over and over in the wakes of the Higgins boats heading in for shore, and men I had seen only moments before, the next time I looked, had vanished suddenly under the waves. Mortar shells and cannonballs were throwing up shrapnel and geysers of water, and I could hear the sound of machine gun and rifle fire in the distance, but I could not see Bobby anywhere and I was getting frantic.

An eternity passed before I finally did see the flood tide carrying his body toward shore. I started swimming after him but I was incredibly tired and for every five strokes I took, I gained only a yard at most. The distance between us closed grudgingly, as if the sea had some prior claim on his soul, and when I finally did catch up to him, I discovered that his head had fallen to one side and was under the water—he appeared to be unconscious. Quickly but gently I lifted his head out of the water and held it up with one hand while wrapping my other arm around his chest, thereby allowing the life jacket to keep us both afloat. The only energy I had to expend was holding Bobby's head above the water and kicking my legs. Nearby, survivors of the explosion were milling around; most had calmed down considerably and were using what strength they had left to tread water. Some had latched onto boards and were calling out for help to the Higgins boats which, having deposited their cargo on the beach, had come back out to rescue the rest of us.

Meanwhile I kept talking to Bobby, trying to revive him. But I wasn't getting any response and I was worried sick. "Talk to me, Bobby," I begged. "You're okay now. The boats are back. We'll get you help real soon."

Then one of the landing craft pulled alongside of us and some of the crew reached over. I got behind Bobby and told them to grab him under the arms, to pull him up while I pushed. Then we heaved. And when Bobby's dripping body rose out of the sea, I saw that both of his legs were gone from above the knees. Not even his pants remained. He must have been dead from the moment he hit the water.

I didn't know what to do. That's when I came apart.

I never did make it to the beach that day. The Higgins boat that picked us up took us out to one of the Navy destroyers where I was placed in the sickbay, suffering, the ship's doctor said, from a cerebral concussion. Maybe because of the head wound, or maybe because nature has a way of protecting a person from painful memories, my mind was a blank for the next twenty-four hours, and the next thing I recall I was on my back on a cot in a field hospital tent in Moresby. I stayed there for several days, chain smoking cigarettes and staring at the canvas ceiling, unable to sleep. At one point I sat down to write Bobby's parents a letter, thinking that might relieve the pain. I wanted to tell them all about Bobby; how much he meant to everybody, particularly me, and how much we all needed him. My head was full of things I wanted to say, but I never did finish the letter. I would have had to tell his parents how he died, and I couldn't do that.

Now I wish I had written that letter. I really wish I had.

On the third day, Harry Blackman stopped in to see me. He sat on a chair beside my cot, smoking while he talked, 240 pounds on a six foot four inch frame. Harry Blackman was regular Army, a World War I veteran, a father figure. He looked embarrassed, fumbled for words, said how much he had admired Bobby, said how sorry he was, sat patiently, silently, while I unloaded all my anger and frustration on him. Then we talked for awhile about Bobby, and, when we were done, Harry said that the guys needed me and that he expected me to return to the unit. I told him what he could do with the unit—that I didn't want to be part of anyone's army anymore. Looking old and weary, Harry sighed and said softly, "You'll come back, Doug," and then he left.

Later that afternoon I found myself walking over to the quartermaster's hut and picking up new equipment—I'd lost everything but my shirt and pants and boots—then reporting back on the line. But I was just going through the motions. Emotionally I was through.

Chapter Three

Our ascent up the south face of the Owen Stanleys carried my unit, by now reduced in size to a single company, through the squalid villages of Ioribaiwa, Nauro Creek, Menari, and Efogi to Myola, site of a sacred Papuan burial ground. Just beyond ghostly Myola, a sky-top mountain pass sat in a valley between two raincloud shrouded peaks. Seventy-five hundred feet above sea level and succinctly called the Gap, this mist-covered, rolling plateau was criss-crossed by a labyrinth of narrow, broken trails, and it was here that the Japanese elected to make their stand.

While General Horii led the main body of the South Seas Detachment on its humiliating retreat to outposts on the north coast of the dragon's tail, a battalion strength unit of crack Japanese troops stayed behind to cover their rear. These seasoned jungle fighters (veterans of Malaya and Rabaul who were commanded by the ruthless Colonel Yazawa) knew better than to meet our advance head-on; instead, they split up into small patrols which scattered throughout the jungle, fading unseen into the dense foliage lining the serpentine trails. And there they waited. It didn't matter that now it was they who were outnumbered and relatively ill-equipped—that didn't mean the job got any easier. Not by a long shot. *They* knew the terrain, *they* had the high ground, and *they* were the ones with their backs to the wall.

As it would for any unit operating under similar conditions, it became necessary for ours to send out scouting patrols to ascertain the strength and position of the enemy. If a scouting party met no resistance, or if it discovered no conclusive evidence of the enemy's whereabouts, standard operating procedure dictated that the main body of troops advance for a prescribed distance, dig in, establish a new defensive perimeter, then dispatch more scouts. This made for slow progress, however, and our commanders were roundly accused of being over-cautious. Let it be known that political considerations based in ignorance alone prompted such unjust criticism; for those of us inching through the malevolent jungle, the task was nothing less than an interminable nightmare. A man on patrol senses that something "out there" is watching him from the shadows. He knows that a predatory beast is dogging him, waiting for him to stumble or fall behind his comrades. A feeling of foreboding eats away at his nerves until.. . .

Scouting patrols are undoubtedly the most hazardous duty a soldier must undertake, and the most dangerous job on any patrol belongs to the point man—the man in front. Not only is the point man a sitting duck for snipers, but he's also incredibly vulnerable to booby traps such as camouflage pits with poison-tipped bamboo stakes implanted on the bottom, or TNT land mines, or wire-trip explosives. It seemed that every day during the forward movement, another point man was listed dead or missing. Every day another patrol returned to base camp smaller than when it departed. And that's why, contrary to the Hollywood version of war, soldiers in their right minds simply do not volunteer for scouting patrols. That's why scouting patrols are conducted strictly on a rotation basis, with everyone at one time or another being obligated to go.

It was a Thursday when my turn came. I know it was a Thursday because Charley said so during a conversation we had early that morning. How he knew, I haven't the foggiest idea; it's just one of those things that sticks out in my mind.

The invisible sun had risen; we knew it had because the mottled half-light of daytime in the jungle was filtering through the intertwined tree-tops, bringing with it a flicker of reassurance. At least we *could* see, through the customary veil of swirling ground mists, the vague forms of our weary comrades emerging from their airless foxholes, stretching their arms and legs and rubbing at the strap of tension that clamps across the neck and shoulders during a night on the line. Believe me, anyone who brags that he can relax in a foxhole, if he isn't lying, is operating on one brain cell out of a billion.

A foul smelling steam rose from our clammy clothes as we

20

wandered back within the perimeter and as fresh men came forward to take our positions. Our faces were caked with mud and grime, and the oxygen-starved air made breathing difficult. The mood in camp was subdued.

As usual, Charley and I headed straight for the mess tent for hot coffee and tepid powdered eggs. But mostly for the coffee. Dysentery caused by stupefying heat and humidity, bad water, rancid food, overflowing latrines and flies, had seen to it that eating was never a major issue. We each opened a can of C-rations, dumped out the contents (spam, hard crackers, chocolate bar pumped full of preservatives), saved only the cigarettes which we greedily smoked while we sipped our coffee. Together the caffeine and smoke worked like a tonic, cutting through my stupor, extracting my dulled senses from the muck and the mire they'd been immersed in all night long, putting me partially back in touch with myself once again. After our morning stimulants we stumbled through our early morning ritual of staking out a piece of dry ground, stripping and ridding each other's body of leeches and worms and such, then cleaning our rifles. The intense heat and humidity were causing the bolt mechanisms in our Springfields to rust, and the steel firing pins actually looked soggy, and they had a tendency to jam unless you cleaned them daily and left a bullet in the breach with the bolt open whenever there was a chance you might need to use your weapon. Which was all the time.

After all that, Charley and I sat down to rest, Charley leaning back against a tree and propping his rifle beside him. I looked at him hard. His eyes were bloodshot from lack of sleep and perpetual shock and he hadn't shaved in days. Although it was still early morning, already his forehead was beading over with sweat. It looked to me like fever.

"You feeling okay?" I asked him. "You don't look so good."

"Yeah, I'm all right," he answered weakly, then added as an afterthought, "aw, fuck it." Which meant that nothing, absolutely nothing, was okay.

"That's what I say," I agreed. At that point, two or three days had elapsed since I had returned to the line from the field hospital tent in Moresby, and Charley had followed me into camp the day after. Incidentally, the landing operation had been a big success. The guys who made it to shore that day, including Charley, did the job—they cleaned the little bastards out of there. Not that it made any difference to Charley or me; what with Bobby and Andy gone, we had both kind of washed our hands of the whole fucking war.

"Remember on the troopship, when they let us up on deck to get initiated into Davy Jones' Locker?" Charley asked.

"Sure," I replied, "how could I forget? We ran the gauntlet and the sailors slapped us with huge sponges dipped in some sort of disgusting smelling fish oil—shit!"

Charley probed deeper. "Remember the dolphins we saw on both sides of the convoy, how they were skimming over the water so fast they passed us going in the same direction?"

"Yeah, I remember. They were beautiful."

"Did you hear the sailors say it was a sign of good luck?" he inquired, wiping the sweat from his eyes with his fist, about to make a point.

"What about it?" I pressed, impatient to know exactly what he was getting at.

"Well, don't fuckin' believe it," Charley said bitterly. "It might be good luck to sailors, but it don't mean shit to us."

With that we both fell into a moody silence, me wrestling with my private demons, Charley sitting back and closing his red, tearful eyes, probably thinking about his wife in St. Louis. She had written to him recently saying that she had been having second thoughts about their marriage. Charley blamed the Army. He had been told by the recruiters at the enlistment center that he could join a unit stateside, but that turned out to be a lie, too. And once he was in, there wasn't a damn thing he could do about it.

"You know what, Doug?" Charley said.

"What now?" I asked, feeling sorry for him.

"Fuck it," he stated flatly. "Fuck the US Army, but most of all, fuck New Guinea."

There were three cigarettes in a C-ration package, and I had just lit up the second one when our platoon leader, Lieutenant Silverman, came over to us and said, "Okay, Valentine.

You are Valentine, right? Okay then. You're on patrol with us today, so get your gear together. Make sure you have two canteens of water, not one, and make sure you draw an extra bandolier of ammunition. We'll form up in 20 minutes. Be there."

Charley and I stared up in disbelief. Silverman was one of those typical "ninety-day wonders" whose only concern was appearing like a 2nd lieutenant in complete control of the situation. He had been somebody's aide down on the beach until a few days before, when he was sent up to the line, and he hadn't wised up at all since then. We had already written him off.

Silverman returned our incredulous stare, mocking us, then demanded to know, completely out of the blue, "What's that on your shirt, Valentine?"; pushing his glasses up on his nose as he spoke. They were always slipping off.

"What?" I mumbled, exhaling a stream of smoke, pretending not to know that he meant the crossed-swords patch I'd sewn over one pocket. I thought it looked dashing.

"That," Silverman whined, pointing. "That goddamned crossed-swords patch on your shirt. Where'd you get it?"

"Got it in Moresby," I said glibly. "Traded it for a Jap flag." I did *not* mention that I had traded it to a guy who was selling captains and lieutenants bars to enlisted men who wanted to masquerade as officers, and I wisely stopped short of asking him if that was where he had gotten his.

"I don't give a damn where you got it, just get rid of it, now!" Silverman was livid, overly so, even though my wearing the patch was technically against the rules. What really upset him was my fuck-it-all attitude. You see, once our officers got up on the line, and the enormity of the situation hit them between the eyes, they quietly removed their coveted bars and assorted symbols of rank, so as not to become targets. Even our sergeants had ripped the hash marks off their shirts.

"Sure, right away, sir," I replied. Charley groaned and muttered, "Asshole officer," as Silverman stomped away.

Morale was very low. All along the line we had lost as many men to our "questers for glory"—bad officers like Silverman who were quite willing to sacrifice a few GIs for the sake of their own advancement—as we had to the Japanese. Don't get me wrong; most of our officers were a minor nuisance we had learned to ignore rather than getting into the inevitable hassle, and we were able to forgive them their fear and stupidity. But we could never forgive our "questers", and we developed an uncontrollable hostility toward *them*. Now, if a "ninety-day wonder" needlessly sent GIs to their death, he paid with his life. It was that simple. The company sergeant got him out behind a tree, and that was the end of it.

"I gotta get ready to go," I said to Charley.

"Yeah," he replied apologetically. "Fuck it."

I wandered over to the quartermaster's hut, drew my extra clips, moved over to the mess tent for fresh water and salt tablets, grabbed some C-ration cans and walked over to where the patrol was forming up. While I waited I smoked my last cigarette. You had to smoke them fast, before they got soggy and disintegrated, like everything else in New Guinea. God how I hated that place.

This was going to be my first patrol and I wasn't happy at all. I'd heard fellows talking who'd already been out. I had seen them shake their heads and sigh the way people do when they can't describe something—something they tell you about with a look in their eyes—and they had all been out with experienced officers. It was just my bad luck, I suppose, but this was going to be Silverman's first time out too; he had absolutely no business leading a patrol, and that sad fact heightened my considerable apprehension.

The patrol was to consist of me, five other GIs, Silverman, and one of our veteran NCOs, Sergeant O'Keefe, at the point. No doubt about it, O'Keefe was the man in charge. He came down the line, dead serious, saying he hoped we'd all shoved something into our stomachs and taken a crap. He told us to watch himself or Silverman for hand signals and to respond accordingly, and if we couldn't see either of them, to watch the man directly in front—that we'd relay all signals down the line. Talking, he stressed, was to be kept at a minimum and there was to be no smoking.

Then O'Keefe suggested that if anyone got separated from the patrol, that the best thing to do was to stop and stay put, rather than foraging around in the forest where it's so easy to lose all sense of direction, to get lost, and to get into deeper trouble. That was only a suggestion, of course; certain situations might arise which would require independent action. But technical advice like that, the type of advice that only experience can qualify someone to dispense, helped a lot. And Sergeant O'Keefe had plenty of experience. Although cynical by nature and not the kind of man to show concern, O'Keefe was extremely sharp, street-wise and army-wise, and he had a reputation for being good when the chips were down. He was big and strong, about thirty-five, married to the Army and liked by us all.

When O'Keefe was finished having words with us, Silverman sauntered down the line to check us out. Lord knows what he expected to see—we all looked pretty ragged around the edges. In the mad rush to get us into action, we hadn't been issued summer weight gear, and it was already insufferably hot out, so some of the guys weren't wearing their shirts. Silverman told them to put them on. I'd left my helmet and poncho behind, figuring that the extra water and ammo were enough weight to drag through the jungle, and I had an uneasy feeling that Silverman was going to give me a hard time about it. Instead, when he reached me he said irritably, "Didn't I tell you to get rid of that goddamned patch?"

"Guess I just forgot, sir," I said testily, looking him straight in the eye. One of the other guys laughed nervously.

"Shit!" Silverman scowled. I could sense his fear.

We moved out of camp single file, Indian fashion, with Sergeant O'Keefe at the point, Lieutenant Silverman following him, and everyone else—Murphy, Walter, Pete, Jackie, Whitey and me—strung out behind. I was the last man in line and all I could think about was how much I despised New Guinea. There were butterflies in the pit of my stomach; from the moment we started tunneling through the ominous jungle twilight, a feeling of claustrophobia gripped me—a feeling of foreboding that brought a constriction to my throat and made

25

me gulp for breath—a feeling that would not let go. There was no path but the one we made, and that was so tight, winding through vegetation so thick, that a Japanese soldier could hide behind a fern leaf two feet away and never be seen. *That* was the scariest part of the fighting in New Guinea—the Japanese were invisible. Occasionally we saw their corpses, but otherwise they were like phantoms slipping silently in between the trees, living in the shadows, blending into the luxuriant foliage like chameleons, wearing the jungle for protection like a suit of green armor.

The distance separating us varied as we went along; in those places where the underbrush was heavy we drew closer together, slowing down and bunching up while O'Keefe and Silverman used their bayonets like machetes to clear the tangled vines and hanging branches away from their faces. When the vegetation thinned out, so did we. At times we moved through dense bamboo stands that shot straight up out of sight, blocking out the sun and casting a sickly yellow glow over the clumps of grass, the saplings and the rhododendrum-type shrubs that covered the ground. At other times we skirted enormous cypress trees, stepping carefully over the cone-shaped outgrowths on their roots. In such places the earth was pitched at sharp angles and we had to clutch at vines and branches to keep our balance, only sometimes pulling away streamers of moss instead, slipping and falling headfirst into the dank, putrid soil. It was disgusting.

It was hard to see more than twenty feet ahead, too, so after every step we listened intently to the perfidious jungle sounds—sounds that could destroy a man. Rain water dripped from over-hanging branches; gusts of wind rustled through the shrubbery; birds shrieked; small leathery lizards scurried beside us or jumped from tree to tree. Even the harmless chirping of tree frogs and crickets became menacing in that evil environment. You had to learn which noises to attend to and which to ignore, for unlike sounds emitted on a city street or in a canyon, sounds in the cushiony jungle are abruptly, mysteriously absorbed and thus impossible to trace. However, once a man was able to distinguish between natural and unnatural noises, and was able to prevent them from expanding his concern, half his problems in that wicked jungle were licked.

The other half were physical and much harder to overcome, and after half an hour of hiking I was completely exhausted. A light rain had begun to fall, making the leaf and humus coated jungle floor incredibly slippery, and I kept stumbling over jutting roots, falling further and further behind the other men. The weight of my Springfield 303 seemed to be dragging me down; it's a long cumbersome weapon, very accurate but eminently unsuited for jungle warfare, where the fighting is up close, often hand-to-hand. A smaller weapon with more fire-power, even if at closer range, would have been more sensible, and I found myself wishing that I had one of the shorter, lighter carbines we'd heard so much about, or even one of the Thompson submachine guns the Aussies carried.

No such luck.

My breath was coming in the short, painful bursts of a sprinter when we took our first break; we'd only been out for about 45 minutes, but it felt to me like we'd been walking forever, to the ends of the earth. My throat was so parched that I couldn't swallow, and that made me nervous, so I reached for my canteen, unscrewed the cap and took a long drink of metallic tasting water, then a couple more. That made me feel much better. I looked around: Silverman and O'Keefe were conferring in whispers up ahead, wrangling over something, but no one else was saying a word. Talking wasted too much energy. We sat in coiled silence, our eyes darting everywhere.

I couldn't believe how tired I was; my bouts with malaria were taking an awful lot out of me. I hadn't expected anything as exhausting as this and I cursed myself for coming back on the line. But of course Bobby was still alive then. Bobby, my best friend and protector, dead at the age of eighteen. I couldn't get over it. I couldn't understand why God would take a truly decent person like him, and allow other men—evil men—to live. And now that Bobby was gone, my reservoir of will seemed to have vanished, too. I'd become an emotionless person, detached, like I was viewing the world through bi-

27

noculars. I knew if he hadn't died, that I would have taken myself out of it, but it was too late for that now. I had to keep my mind on the present situation. That's the secret, I reminded myself. Take it moment to moment.

Ten minutes after we stopped, we picked up where we'd left off, and ten minutes after that I was spent. The air was laden with pollen and mold, and breathing hurt. I just couldn't keep up with the others. We were moving steadily uphill and the further we traveled away from our perimeter, the more I was seized by feelings of terror and isolation. I kept wondering, "When are we going to turn back? How is this asshole Silverman ever going to find the way home? For all I know, we could be traveling in circles!"

The terrain never seemed to change. What I saw ten minutes earlier—green dripping vegetation alive with swarming insects—looked exactly like what I was seeing now. And on and on. There were no distinguishing landmarks I could point to, or use as a reference, or say about with any certainty, "I'll remember this hollow tree, or that configuration of rocks on the way back, so I'll know where I've been and where I'm going." There was nothing but a riot of green—of trees and leaves and ferns and vines.

Paramount in my mind was keeping the man in front of me, Whitey, in sight at all times, but at times that was impossible; the jungle had a devious knack for swallowing him up at every twist and turn. "Christ," I said to myself. "Supposing I let them get too far ahead and I get lost? What am I going to do out here all alone? I don't know how to get back. I don't even have a compass! What in the world am I going to do?" And of course we were trying to be just as quiet as we could, so I didn't dare call out to Whitey to wait, although I wanted to desparately. My vision was blurred by sweat and tears and a hundred stinging insect bites all around my eyes, and then there was a cloudburst and I lost sight of Whitey through a curtain of rain. Sometimes twenty or thirty seconds would elapse before I saw him. I experienced moments of abject panic. I'd think, "I'm lost! My God, I'm lost!"

Chapter Four

If we hadn't taken a second break, I don't know what I would have done—the intense heat and humidity were utterly unbearable and my exhaustion was complete. My arms and legs felt like lead. My hands and face were cut and stinging from grabbing at the thorny vines and branches that lined the twisting, ever-rising path we hacked through the jungle. My head was swimming, my lungs were on fire, and I had lost my concentration, all of which amounted to trouble. Never in my life had I felt so bone tired. I looked around; the other guys were tired, too, I could see that, but they weren't as bad off as me and that made me nervous. I was drained of fluids from pushing through the sweltering underbrush (the temperature was well over 100 degrees) so I took a few more swigs from my canteen. That finished it. I had one left. Another reason for concern.

Sergeant O'Keefe eased his way gingerly down the line, whispering words of encouragement, warning us to stay alert, to go easy on the water ("You'll need it more later on," he said to me), to keep each other in sight and to tighten up the formation from there on in. He seemed unusually restive. We nodded that we had heard. Then O'Keefe moved back up the line to Lieutenant Silverman, who was standing, leaning against a tree, looking down at the ground and trying to catch his breath. His face was white and he jumped when O'Keefe tapped him on his shoulder. Silverman nodded, O'Keefe motioned for everyone to stand, and we moved out once again.

Getting up was a hard thing to do; I found myself wishing that Bobby was there to help me out, my mind drifting back to all the times in the past that he'd been there when I needed him.

But that was ages ago—I had to rely on myself now. Memories were too much empty baggage to carry on patrol, I reminded myself. They were painfully distracting, and I had to stay alert.

Just then we picked up a winding trail that moved gradually downhill. Hiking became easier. Naturally I assumed that Silverman had been looking for that particular trail all along, but I wasn't positive, and I don't think Silverman was either. Not that it made any difference—in a matter of minutes we broke out of the steaming, dripping jungle into a field of hip-high kunai grass. Invisible birds squawked an alarm. We could see the leaves rustling where they'd fluttered into the tree-tops.

Suddenly the sun was in the sky. Seemed like we hadn't seen it in days. From this position I judged it to be around noon, maybe later. It was *hot* in the open. I felt exposed. The hairs on the back of my neck bristled. I sensed danger.

A solitary plane flew overhead; I looked but couldn't see it. Bombers fly in squadrons, I recalled, must be reconnaissance.

Breathing was easier in the field. The air was thinner, and there were fewer flies and mosquitoes. A gentle breeze swept over the golden field, bending the razor-sharp blades of kunai grass across the footpath so that they sliced across the back of my hands, drawing blood. For some strange reason the breeze reminded me of my Aunt Gertie's dairy farm in Danbury. I felt like we were a million miles from nowhere.

We moved quickly once we were in the open, momentarily revitalized, eager to get into the protective cover of the brush. Sergeant O'Keefe was approximately 75 feet in front of me, with everyone else spaced evenly in between. It'd been half an hour since our last break.

Then we entered the jungle again, slowing down and bunching up, feeling familiar fingers of fear clutch at our throats. We continued for less than five minutes across a relatively level stretch where the trail straightened out then heaved gently upwards into a solid wall of darkness. The vegetation was very heavy on both sides, but the trail was flat and straight and I could see clearly right up to O'Keefe. The trail began to rise where he was at, and that's when they hit us.

The Japanese must have known that our patrols were using that trail, because they were ready and waiting in concealed positions in the trees and behind the bushes at a point where it was straight and moving slightly uphill—the perfect place for an ambush. The moment we were inextricably within their trap, they showered us with concussion and fragmentation grenades. All hell broke loose. I heard rifle fire and explosions up ahead, followed by anguished screams. Then a terrific blast of heat flew into my face and encompassed my body, knocking me backwards off my feet like a swipe from a giant hand.

I was lying on my back when I came to, stunned and disoriented but able to hear hysterical screaming and wailing through the thunder in my ears. My brain reeled from the blow I'd been dealt and my body from the neck down seemed paralyzed. I was gagging on blood in my nose, throat and mouth, and blood was oozing out of my ears. Above, the green mesh of tree-tops and leaves spun crazily—I closed my eyes to keep from being sick. Then, with an immense effort that called upon all my strength, I raised my head and opened my eyes. What I saw was horrifying beyond human comprehension. Japanese soldiers were sliding down from the trees and emerging from the underbrush on both sides of the trail, chattering and chirping like a bunch of excited monkeys. I watched spellbound as groups of three and four began running up and down the line of maimed and wounded men, smiling, gloating, moving in for the kill.

My vision was distorted and for some reason I could see more clearly in the distance than I could up close. From my position at the rear of the patrol I could see Sergeant O'Keefe, Lieutenant Silverman and the third man in line, Murphy. The rest was a blur, slowly coming into focus. O'Keefe was sprawled on his back, his left arm blown completely away, his head rolling from side to side, but he was conscious and screaming out in pain and terror. A group of four Japanese soldiers pounced on him, plunging their bayonets deep into his face, chest and stomach.

As much as I wanted to, as hard as I tried, I couldn't coordinate my thoughts with my body. I couldn't move.

The Japanese started working their way down the line, gathering next around Lieutenant Silverman, who'd taken a hit in the chest but who was also conscious and desperately pleading, "Please don't! My God! Please don't do it to me!" He'd seen what happened to Sergeant O'Keefe. But the Japanese bastards paid no attention to him. They did the same thing to him and they did the same thing to everyone else.

"Oh my God!" I realized, so consumed by terror that I thought my heart was going to explode, "They're going to do the same thing to me!" My eyes were riveted on the four Japanese soldiers coming at me—the same ones who were doing the dirty work—but I couldn't turn away. I couldn't move my arms or legs. "Please God," I prayed, "let me die before they reach me!"

By then more Japanese soldiers were joining in the slaughter. They were pulling the pants off the dead men, laughing and giggling like it was a picnic for the fucks; then chopping the pricks and testicles off the corpses and stuffing them in the breathless mouths.

I wasn't sure that what I was seeing was real. But it was! It was actually happening!

Then everything fell sharply into focus. Time flattened out. The four Japanese soldiers coming at me seemed to move in slow motion. They clustered around me with their rifles raised in the air, blood dripping from their bayonets onto my chest. I looked up at them and they looked down at me. "Why don't they get it over with?" I asked myself, too frightened to even beg for my life.

At that exact moment one of the Japanese soldiers, their commanding officer I assume, held his hand up, signalling the others to halt. He pointed at my chest, uttered a guttural command. One of the lower ranking Japanese soldiers spun his rifle around in his hands and smashed the butt end down hard on my sternum. I gasped. Having taken that precaution, they huddled together to discuss what to do with me.

Seconds later the one who had hit me reached into his hip pocket, pulled out a filthy bandana, tied my hands in front of me and pulled me to my feet. The concussion from the grenade had destroyed my equilibrium; my knees wobbled and I could barely stand. I knew I must. A searing pain shot through my chest. Bolts of lightning flashed and claps of thunder boomed in my head. Visually I was in and out and what I could see was shrouded in a red mist of pain.

The Japanese patrol formed up in single file, with me in the middle, then moved out quickly, leaving behind a line of seven mutilated corpses as a testament to their unspeakable savagery. Where they were taking me, or what they were planning to do with me, I had no idea. I was consumed by panic.

From before dawn to after dusk for the next two days, I was half-pushed, half-dragged through the jungle, at every step expecting to be shot or stabbed or heinously tortured. Based on horror stories I'd heard from Australians, I thought the Japanese were going to pull out my fingernails or stick bamboo slivers in my ears. Christ, I'd seen for myself what they were capable of doing and I simply could not imagine why I'd been taken alive. We'd been assured that the enemy never took prisoners, which is the main reason why, on the evening prior to the forward move, all the enlisted men in my outfit had taken off their dogtags and thrown them in a pile—on the off-chance that if you were captured, but couldn't be identified, you might be considered important and kept alive. That's why I wasn't wearing my dogtag on patrol; but then again, neither was anyone else. So why was I still alive?

At the time I assumed that Japanese officers traveled at the rear of their own patrols and that I'd been mistaken for an Intelligence officer and was wanted for questioning. But even that explanation was hard to swallow, and it wasn't until several days later that it finally dawned on me that the Japanese officer who'd spared my life was pointing at the crossed-swords patch on my shirt—the one Lieutenant Silverman had told me to remove. Obviously I can only assume that that's the answer; I had absolutely no way of knowing what they were talking about or what influenced them to take me prisoner. At the time I expected to be killed on the spot; after that, nothing made sense. Nothing but my hidden rage and the knowledge that I was in mortal danger.

We'd been led to believe that the Japanese weren't well

armed, but they were, and the reality of their preparedness shocked me. I couldn't take my eyes off their weapons as we moved through the jungle. Some carried knee mortars, some held small calibre rifles, and others had clumsy looking machine guns. They were all outfitted in summer-weight tan uniforms with peaked caps (no helmets), baggy pants that resembled knickers, and high lacing boots. They looked like and acted like professional soldiers, self-assured and well disciplined, never speaking once we began to move. And they knew precisely where they were going.

I couldn't stop comparing them to us. Hell, half of our men didn't wear their shirts because of the wicked heat and humidity, and hardly anyone wore his helmet unless we were under mortar fire. I hadn't been wearing mine on the patrol. Each man had his own individual style in our army—no two men looked alike. But the Japanese dressed the same and behaved the same and that added to my concern. We'd been assured that they'd been reduced to drinking polluted water, to eating tree bark, grass and roots. Not so. Not at all. The Japanese were light on their feet, fast and fit; it was an efficient unit, not a run-down force that had captured me, and that made me nervous, too.

At intervals along the way I was shoved to the ground and fresh troops would take over custody, the new guards invariably kicking me and clubbing me, doing their damndest to make me walk faster; enjoying it too. Only once was I permitted to eat, and I managed very little sleep at night.

On the third day I was blindfolded. Up until then we'd been moving steadily downhill, on the far side of the Owen Stanleys, but now the earth beneath my feet changed from dirt to sand, leveled-out, and my captors relaxed and began speaking in normal tones, no longer the urgent whispers of the front. For the next several hours I was pushed and shoved along the beach, stumbling every few steps because of the blindfold, swooning under the furnace heat of the equatorial sun, and sensing, all around me, a great deal of activity. I guessed that we were at one of the principal Japanese bases on the north coast of New Guinea; Buna, perhaps, or Gona.

Wherever we were, the minute we stopped walking a rifle butt struck me hard on the left side of my head, my knees gave out and I crumbled into the sand, semi-conscious.

When my senses returned I heard, through the roar reverberating in my skull, the sputter and cough of a small outboard motor starting up nearby, and I could hear the gentle sound of water lapping against a pier. Someone dragged me to my feet, manhandled me across a sagging wooden plank into a small craft (the one I'd heard starting up) and we proceeded to chug-a-lug out to a larger vessel, the smell of its burnt, oil-coated decks leading me to believe that it was a merchant ship of some sort. Once aboard I was taken down below decks into a hold in the forward part of the ship—I could tell where I was located by my relationship to the drone of the engines, which are always midship. My blindfold was removed and I was propelled into a tiny room filled with coiled hawsers. The door was bolted behind me.

It was pitch black in that stifling, unventilated cell; my head throbbed, my chest ached, I was exhausted and famished and roasting alive, and I had to sit perfectly still, like a Buddha, to keep from fainting. But I was glad to be alone. Taking off my shirt, I used the sleeve to wipe the caked blood off my face and out of my ears, and then I tried to collect my badly disjointed thoughts; however, each time I shut my eyes to rest, I envisioned the anguished faces of the seven men on patrol. I saw their terror and I saw them die. Even when my eyes were open they stared at me from the infernal darkness of my cell, saying, "We died, but you lived." I felt I had no right to be alive. I didn't expect to be alive much longer.

The terrible nightmares which were to haunt me in years to come (not immediately, but several years after the war was over—what's now called delayed stress syndrome) had their birth in the stifling bowels of that mysterious ship. Although I'd never again know fear of death, the ferocity of those little Japanese monsters having driven all vestiges of reverence for my own life completely out of my mind, neither would I ever again know peace of mind. The faces of those seven men would be my constant companions; along with Bobby's, and Andy's, and those of a hundred others.

When the Japanese cargo ship I was in reached its destination I was blindfolded once more, led up a series of stairs, steel ladders and hatches from the hold to the upper deck, then prodded down a gangway and into an open vehicle. I didn't know where I was and, having lost all track of time in the emptiness of my tiny cell, I was very confused. Altogether I'd counted fourteen meals, each one consisting of a cold ball of rice which I ate from my palm with my fingers, plus a cup of water, about half a pint; but I still didn't know if I'd been fed once or twice a day, so I wasn't sure if the voyage had lasted seven or fourteen days. It's impossible to accurately calculate the passage of time when you're trapped in total darkness, and only when they slipped my meals through the slot in the cell door could I see light. Just to add insult to injury, the bastards never emptied my slop bucket; I was crawling with lice and I stank to high heaven.

We drove for approximately half an hour at a slow rate of speed, first along a wharf (I could feel the refreshing sea breeze and hear fishing boats groaning against their moorings in the harbor), then along the outskirts of a city (twangy Oriental voices and street sounds—no cars) and eventually into open country. Throughout the ride my guards spoke continually to one another but I didn't recognize their voices and I knew they weren't the sailors who'd been watching and feeding me aboard ship. But they were carefree and laughing and their complacency increased my suspicion, and my dread, that I was on mainland Japan.

My knowledge of the geography of the Far East was about what you'd expect from a ninth grade dropout—negligible— as was my understanding of the Japanese people, the little I knew about either having been fed to me by the Army in various forms of propaganda, most of which I intuitively mistrusted. My ignorance, in any case, contributed to my apprehension. I'd heard that the Japanese considered capture an unpardonable sin and a fate worse than death; that any Nipponese soldier who was even inadvertently captured by the enemy automatically forfeited all claims to manly honor, was doomed to a life of shame (as was his family), and that the poor fellow would even be barred from entering Japanese heaven. I'd also heard that in accordance with this Spartan philosophy the Japanese treated their own prisoners of war with uncompromising cruelty and contempt. I was very dejected and I felt sure they were plotting to put me on public display, to debase and to humiliate me. My spirits were at rock bottom.

The vehicle came to a sudden stop; the guards grabbed me, pulled me out of the truck and threw me viciously on the ground. As I struggled to my feet I heard them yelling to someone, and then, to my amazement, I heard a man's voice responding to them in English, with an unmistakable Australian accent. The force of the words nearly knocked me off my feet again—I was so startled that I failed to register what was being said. Although I could distinctly hear other Australian voices in the background, I still wasn't able to figure out where I was.

The man who had answered walked slowly to me, placed his hand firmly on my shoulder, and said in typical Aussie style, breezy and casual, "Hi, Yank. Let's get rid of that blindfold for you." I could tell from the extemporaneous tone of his voice that he had not been expecting me—that he must have been notified of my arrival at that particular instant—and yet he was handling the situation with uncanny confidence. Stepping lightly behind me, he untied the blindfold and let it slip away, but, having been wrapped in total darkness for days on end, my eyes were hyper-sensitive to the sunlight and when the cloth slipped away and the intense glare stabbed my eyes, I automatically cried out and covered them with my hands.

"You've got a bit of a problem there, Yank," the Australian remarked sympathetically. "We'll deal with that in a little while, but first, let's find a home for you here."

"Where is here?" I asked. "Who are you?"

"I'm Lieutenant Duffy," he replied matter-of-factly, "but all the guys call me Duff." As he said that, I heard the truck turn around and drive away, at which point Duff took me by the arm and led me in the direction of the Australian voices. Once more I asked him where I was.

Nonchalantly, as if my whereabouts was irrelevant, he said,

"Oh, you're on the island of Leyte in the Philippines, just outside the town of Tacloban. You're in a Japanese prisoner-of-war camp along with 120 Australian and 44 British soldiers." Both names—Leyte and Tacloban—drew a blank. I had no idea where I was. But, as we walked deeper into the camp compound, I could hear the Aussies calling out to me, saying, "How ya doing, Yank?" and "Welcome to the Hotel Tacloban," and a sense of security began to take root and grow within me. It was good to hear their cocky, irreverent voices, and for the first time in days the recurrent pangs of loneliness and despair began to fade, replaced by curiosity and a feeling of awkwardness.

Duff led me inside an enclosure and said crisply, "Here's your pad, Yank. Just sit down, all right? I'll be more specific later on, after you're settled in and your eyes have grown accustomed to the light. In the meantime, the fellows here will help you get your bearings." I could sense several men moving around in the hut as I sank to the floor, sitting cross-legged on a reed mat; after that began the laying-on of hands that served as my reception to POW life. Someone knelt beside me, rubbed my head with a callused hand and said in a pleasing Scottish burr, "You're among friends now, laddie." That was Travis. Another man put his hand on my shoulder, left it there as a sign of camaraderie, then said, "Well, mate, yer all right now, ar'nt ye?" That was Jassy.

"Sure," I said, smiling, feeling safe enough, finally, to lower my guard. With that, other men started touching me and introducing themselves, although I still couldn't squint to see what they looked like. Not until the next day would I be able to form my first visual impressions of the Hotel Tacloban.

Chapter Five

Located approximately 2,000 miles northwest of Port Moresby, Leyte Province is one of several medium sized islands in the Central Philippines called the Visayans; Visayan being the proper name ascribed to both the aboriginal people inhabiting these islands, as well as to the Malayan language they speak. Approximately 115 miles long, north to south, and fifteen to fifty miles wide, east to west, Leyte is inhabited by about 900,000 people, most of whom are very poor. The somewhat larger island of Samar is Leyte's immediate neighbor to the north, located half a mile away across the San Juanico Strait, and Mindanao, the second largest island in the Philippine Archipelago after Luzon, sits twenty-five miles to the south. To the east is the Pacific Ocean; Cebu Island lies directly to the west.

Leyte's capital and principal city, Tacloban (population 30,000) is situated on the island's northeastern corner at the southeastern entrance to the San Juanico Strait in an area that is reclaimed ocean, very fertile, and highly cultivated. A thriving commercial center, Tacloban was of interest to the Japanese for two reasons: first, a small airstrip of great strategic military value sat five miles away on the tip of Cataisan Point; and secondly, Tacloban boasted a sizable port capable of harboring a dozen merchant vessels of average size. The POW camp we called the Hotel Tacloban was located about two miles due west of Tacloban in the midst of a hot and humid plain that drained the entire Leyte Valley and the mountain range visible in the west.

Because it had a good-sized harbor and an airfield, the generals in Tokyo recognized that Tacloban was of the utmost importance militarily. Therefore, in May, they dispatched several thousand troops of the infamous Sixteenth Division (reknowned for the pleasure they took in murdering POWs on the Bataan Death March), along with an engineer regiment (to patch up the roads and docks), to seize control of the city. Which is exactly what happened. This veteran Japanese contingent chased whatever opposition it could find up into the hills, terrorized the residents of Tacloban into submission, then discovered there was nothing left to do. Subsequently, most of them were soon transferred to hot-spots in the South Pacific where the need for combat troops was far more urgent. To fill the power vacuum created by their departure, reluctant Filipino collaborationists were recruited to police Tacloban and to hold at bay, with predictably poor results, their rebellious brothers who had scampered off into the hills.

About the methods and motives of the guerrillas there is much divergence of opinion; among their ranks were stranded American soldiers and sailors who, if you were to ask them, would claim straight-faced to have won the war single-handedly. But the fact of the matter is this: when they weren't battling with rival guerrilla gangs, they were busy extorting and stealing from the civilian population, whom they considered traitors and on whom they had declared war. Furthermore, guerrillas rarely harassed Japanese patrols, and when it did happen it was usually by accident and always with dire consequences. For every Japanese soldier picked-off by guerrillas, the Japanese retaliated by murdering ten innocent Filipinos at random. The residents of Tacloban implicitly mistrusted and feared the guerrillas. Like the U. S. Naval blockade imposed later in the war, guerrilla activity hurt the Filipinos worse than it hurt the Japanese.

Make no mistake about it, the Filipinos were in sorry shape long before the Japanese moved in, with living conditions in Tacloban leaving much to be desired. The city itself was nothing more than a shantytown of *nipa* huts, dingy shacks, a row of ramshackle wooden warehouses along the wharf, one dilapidated Masonic Temple, and half a dozen Spanish style villas—remnants of the colonial past. Hell, the streets were open sewers. But once the Japanese set up shop the situation rapidly deteriorated and the residents soon began to starve. Those who could fled the city for the outlying barrios. Those who could not quickly learned the art of hoarding. But not everyone suffered; as in any beseiged city, pirates and smugglers and blackmarketeers did very well for themselves, profiting from the misfortune of others.

In an effort to win public support for themselves, as well as to legitimize their presence, the Japanese did permit existing elected officials to continue administering the provincial government based in Tacloban. But placating the impatient Japanese proved impossible and when widespread Filipino cooperation was not immediately forthcoming, the Japanese launched a concerted reign of terror to facilitate the process. Crimes perpetrated on the defenseless Filipinos ranged from slapping and otherwise humiliating the men in public, to looting, raping, and murdering with impunity.

All in all, the totalitarian Japanese made their authoritarian American predecessors seem mild in comparison. Those Filipinos who willingly accepted Asian brotherhood and bowed to benevolent Japanese despotism, became grateful beneficiaries of the Greater East Asia Co-Prosperity Sphere. Those who balked lived in perpetual fear of their sadistic overlords. There was no law and there was no justice, and the vast majority of Filipinos had no other choice than to submit.

Among this plethora of divided loyalties there was one topic, at least, upon which everybody in and around Tacloban was in complete accord; all Filipinos, regardless of political affiliation, were well aware that the prisoner-of-war camp two miles due west of town was strictly off-limits. Even the local dogs were smart enough to avoid the Hotel Tacloban.

The Hotel Tacloban was shaped roughly like a trapezoid, the west side approximately 150 yards long and running parallel to the shorter east side, which was about fifty yards in length and bisected by the main gate. The divergent north and south sides each extended for close to two hundred yards and the entire camp compound was enclosed by a seven-and-a-half foot high barbed wire fence. Prisoners were not permitted within ten feet of this boundary line.

Beginning at a point about sixty feet from the eastern side, a row of nine evenly spaced, thatch-roofed huts lined (for about sixty yards) the south side of camp; ten similar huts lined the north side. These primitive hovels, which housed the prison inmates, were a fraction over six feet apart, and each one was about twenty-five feet from the barbed wire. The first hut on the north side—the hut closest to the main gate—was occupied by three Australian officers; Lieutenent Duffy, Lieutenent Simms, and Lieutenent Spaulding. I was quartered in the second hut on that side along with eight Aussie enlisted men (EMs.) The next four huts on the north side were also occupied by between eight and twelve Aussies each, and the final three huts were home for an approximate number of British EMs.

The first hut on the south side of camp served as our infirmary; it was twice as large as any other enclosure and usually contained about two dozen men, all of whom were gravely ill with malaria, dysentery, pneumonia, malnutrition, assorted injuries and wounds, any number of unidentifiable tropical diseases, and psychological disorders. The following five huts on that side belonged to Australian EMs.

In keeping with the sacred traditions of the English Army, which state that under no circumstances are officers of field rank (major and above) expected to cohabitate with junior officers, the very last hut on the south side of camp was the private domain of the ranking British officer, the POW Camp Commandant, Major R. L. Cumyns. Naturally, the second to last hut on that side was occupied by the Major's four commissioned junior officers; Lt. Downey, two 2nd lieutenants, and one sub-altern. The third hut from the end belonged to a dozen or so stalwart British EMs who served to insulate the genteel, refined English officers from the low and mean, unruly Australians.

The Japanese Camp Commandant, Captain Yoshishito, resided with his staff of junior officers in a white-washed, cinderblock building abutting the western end of camp, just south of center. Two dozen or so surly Japanese guards were billeted in a similarly stark building on the western edge of camp, just north of center. Fifty yards of open space separated the Japanese from their solitary American, 44 British, and 120 Australian prisoners.

The only other permanent structure in the Hotel Tacloban

had been placed squarely in the center of the prison yard in the empty space between the last two British huts on either side and the Japanese billets, and was called the Doghouse by the Australians. Made of a durable wood resembling teak, unventilated and only four feet cubed, it was there that POWs were sent for punishment. Our cemetery was located in the area between the guard's billet and the last British hut on the north side of camp.

The long and narrow, twelve by thirty foot huts (cages, really) we lived in were uniformly alike. Having been designed and constructed by Filipinos for use by Filipinos (originally, to incarcerate those Filipinos serving under Lt. Col. Theodore Cornell, the US Army commander in Leyte), they required any Caucasian male of average height to stoop beneath the gently sloping roofs unless he was standing dead center. The structures were made out of bamboo poles covered by thin, dry, faded gold *nipa* fronds, and each hut had two entrances— one to the prison yard, and one facing the fence. There were no doors. In addition, each hut was circumscribed by a two-foot high opening beginning about two-and-a-half feet off the ground, which enabled the refreshing evening breeze to circulate within. Unfortunately, it also allowed the wind to blow in the rain.

The huts were not equipped with floors and we were obliged to sleep without bedding of any sort on musty reed mats spread on the spongy, clay-like ground. These mats had also been designed for diminutive Filipinos and measured less than four feet long and one-and-a-half feet wide. So as not to compete for air, we slept head to foot, lengthwise across the huts, curled up in fetal positions; if you stretched out straight at night in your sleep, you kicked the man behind you in the head. And what with the ground perenially damp and crawling with insects, and our legs dangling uncomfortably over the bottom of the mats, unless a man was totally exhausted, the best that could be hoped for was a fitful night's rest.

Outside the huts the surface of the ground was coated with a fine layer of chalky-white dust resembling talcum powder, which puffed up in tiny clouds if you stomped your foot on it. Beneath this layer of dust, the ground was as hard and reflective as a concrete sidewalk in the city on a bright summer's day, magnifying the sunlight and the heat and creating an intense, distracting glare. Grass grew nowhere within the confines of the barbed wire fence, further augmenting the harsh, barren aspect of the prison camp, and no one, not even the English (contrary to the famous lyric) ventured outside to stand and bake beneath the colossal midday sun.

Nevertheless, despite the occasional typhoon, the climate in Leyte was much milder than it had been in equatorial New Guinea. More often than not the weather was hot and humid, with rain storms occurring daily from July through November, with the temperatures rarely falling below 75 degrees; when it did, we shivered and felt cold. As a matter of practicality we learned to walk slowly, patterning our behavior on the Filipino "manana" model, drifting inexorably into the sluggish rhythm of the tropics. Daylight lasted for an average of thirteen hours, a fact which took me over a year to realize.

The land surrounding the Hotel Tacloban was tediously flat except in the west where undulating, azure mountains reminiscent of the Berkshires in Massachusetts gradually rose in the distance. Foot high patches of elephant grass dotted the landscape, along with low-lying marshes and the numerous, fallow rice-paddies that stretched out monotonously in every direction. Visual contact with the outside world was limited to a bend in Highway 1 (the cowpath leading to Tacloban) at the eastern end of camp. Traffic on the road ranged from light to none at all and consisted almost exclusively of pedestrians; in as much as gasoline was reserved for the military, the few vehicles to be seen belonged to the Japanese Army. The few Filipinos we saw used donkeys or domesticated *carabao* to haul their loads, and even our guards, when they sought entertainment and sake in Tacloban, were compelled to walk.

Life flowed beyond our grasp at the Hotel Tacloban; even the indigent Filipinos travelling Highway 1 were prohibited from stopping or looking inside the barbed wire. There was very little rubber-necking and when it did occur the guards would yell hysterically, flail their arms, point their rifles and scare away anyone who was foolish enough to get caught peeking. Only the pious Franciscans descending from their monastery in the western hills were clever enough to make eye contact with us, communicating furtive, compassionate glances from behind the cowls on their long brown frocks. Otherwise we lived in a vacuum. Although the landscape was flat, we could see neither the sea nor Tacloban, nor were any habitations visible from camp. We *could* see an occasional Japanese transport plane landing or taking off from Cataisan Point airstrip, but it was impossible to see the planes once they had landed and were parked on the ground.

Change was limited to sunrise and sunset, rain or shine. We had no electricity, no plumbing, no clocks, no calendars—the date was a matter of contention. At first each hut had a man marking days, but if the man came down with fever, or dysentery, or whatever, he necessarily lost count, and soon the day of the week became a moot point. Tropical inertia and lethargy triumphed in the end, and time, in any case, stood still behind barbed wire. Like shipwrecked sailors stranded on some desert isle, we were utterly sealed off from the outside world; we were as far removed from our hopes and homes as we were from the mountains on the huge tropical moon.

Chapter Six

My first night at the Hotel Tacloban was a classic study in contrasts; although overcome by a feeling of relief at having survived and fallen in among friends, I was, at the same time, virtually blind, badly disoriented, and totally dumbfounded by the Australian version of English, which bubbles over with pleasant-sounding yet unrecognizable aboriginal words relating to places and things peculiar to Australia. I hadn't been able to follow half of what the men in my hut had said that first night, so I was greatly relieved when Duff came to see me the following morning to explain to me more fully the nature of my new comrades. Not the sort of man to encourage misunderstanding by using 200 words when two would suffice, he ushered me into the center of the prison yard and said, as he made a sweeping gesture with his hand, "What we have here is 120 cowboys." I was careful to note that he made no reference to the British prisoners.

Duff's succinct statement about his countrymen needs little elaboration; just like the mythological, 19th century American cowboy, the Australian bushman was indeed an incorrigible maverick, most likely a farmer or ranch hand or maybe just a drifter. Whatever his chosen occupation, you could be sure that he loved smoking and drinking, cursing and fighting, and doing whatever he damn well pleased—just like a cowboy. And yet, as I soon came to discover, Aussies and Americans are as unalike as kangaroos and buffalo, boomerangs and tomahawks. Starting with their language, Australians possess innumerable cultural idiosyncrasies, all of which they passionately defend as absolutely essential to their national identity. For, first and foremost, Australians are fiercely patriotic.

At times, though (without being facetious), that fierce patriotism is hard to fathom, especially when you consider that Australians are the luckless owners of an inhospitable continent which requires nine-tenths of its population to live within twenty miles of the coastline, mostly along the Eastern Highlands. The greater portion of Australia's desolate and deserted interior, The Outback, is flat and dry and hellishly hot—in a word, unfit for human habitation. Thus there is a marked tendency among Australians to view all foreigners (Americans in particular) with suspicion and envy. Contributing to this sense of xenophobic inferiority is the sad fact that Asian civilizations were aware of Australia's existence for centuries, but chose to ignore it, allowing its aborigines and marsupials to live in harmonious anonymity until the late 18th century, when the British decided to colonize the continent with English and Irish convicts. From that rather inauspicious inception Australians developed an understandably defensive posture about their uninviting homeland (one could even go so far as to say that they were hyper-sensitive about the subject), and I learned very quickly not to brag too much about bountiful America at the Hotel Tacloban.

From what I'd seen in New Guinea, where the Aussies were present in force, the average Australian soldier did indeed carry a chip on his shoulder when it came to Yanks. I'd never dealt with their kind before and, to tell the truth, I didn't particularly like them. Despite the fact that we were there to help them out, they affected a superior attitude. The Aussies thought American soldiers were sissies. "Spoiled kids," they said. And maybe to a certain extent they were right. *They* were the ones fighting an avenging battle in defense of their homeland, not us, and that's precisely why *they* were willing to match the Japanese in terms of ruthlessness.

I must admit that I was shocked, at first, at how brutal the Aussies could be. Case in point: on one occasion in New Guinea, Bobby and Charley and I passed a group of bearded Aussies sitting in a circle in the rain, alternately cursing the Nips and the bloody Brits (to know the Aussies is to know they can't complete a sentence without interjecting several choice profanities), and sharpening their hunting knives on a portable grindstone—they were very good with the blade. One of the Australians was armed with a Bren gun (a type of submachine gun) and he had a Japanese sniper trapped in a nearby tree. Prior to that, from his tree-top vantage point, the sniper had commanded a clear view of the track where it opened up at a cutback, and he'd picked off a few of the Aussie's mates, knowing full well that, for himself, there was no escape. However, fearing a fate worse than death should he fall into Aussie hands, the doomed sniper had tied himself into the tree with a short length of rope. By the time we appeared on the scene, his rifle had fallen to the ground, he was badly wounded, and he was screaming his lungs out in pain and terror. The Aussie with the Bren gun toyed with the sniper for thirty minutes before finishing him off; the coup de grace left the bugger dangling from his perch.

Eventually I came to see that that particular Aussie's cruelty was but a gut reaction to the official Japanese policy of waging the war with such ferocity that we'd roll over and play dead. This policy, which condoned all manner of beastly atrocities, including cannibalism, grossly underrated the fighting spirit of American soldiers. It was only in the very beginning that we were surprised and offended by the Australian capacity for vengeance; it was a very nasty war, and we quickly caught on.

Another interesting difference between Americans and Australians, one which may well explain the Aussie's predisposition toward violence, is that Americans by tradition trace their roots to those Puritanical seekers of religious freedom, the Pilgrims, whereas Aussies tend to think of themselves as descendents of a cruel and corrupt English judicial system (which existed solely to protect the rich) which exiled tens of thousands of their forefathers and foremothers, as slave-laborers, to their shores. Is it any wonder then that the typical Australian relates to the anti-hero? Or that, by nature unreconciled to his station in the overall scheme of things, he harbors a deep and abiding mistrust of authority? Or that, as a soldier, he makes notoriously poor cannon fodder? From what I saw at the Hotel Tacloban, the average Australian believed in his instincts, not his officers. English officers in particular held little sway over the skeptical Australian sensibility, nor did obedience and discipline rate as virtues to be cultivated and preserved by the critical, non-conformist Australian soldier.

Honor was purely a matter of machismo; physical strength and courage were the qualities held in highest esteem. The longer a man could stand on his feet at work, the more abuse his body could absorb, the higher his rank and status among his fellow Australians. The capacity to endure all manner of suffering and hardship without complaint was the true measure of a man's merit.

Holding fast to this manly credo, each and every Aussie at the Hotel Tacloban had carved out his own private space, and any infringement on it, whether intentional or not, was just cause for a fight. Accidentally kicking dirt on another man's pad, or sitting on it without the owner's express consent, or bumping into someone while standing on line for rice—any of these trivial things could easily lead to a brawl. Of course, stern Japanese discipline and punishment had everyone seething with rage and frustration anyway, so only the slightest provocation was ever required to set someone off. When you had to take a slap in the face from some pipsqueak Japanese guard without losing your cool (a defiant grin could lead to a stint in the Doghouse, striking back could lead to far worse), you naturally looked for someplace safe to vent your anger. And the Japanese weren't overly concerned if we fought among ourselves, so the Aussies made full use of that liberty.

Let me remind you that I was still only sixteen—very impressionable and very wet behind the ears—when I checked into the Hotel Tacloban. It was almost forty years ago, and I'm not at all certain that Australians today are anything like they were back then. Most of the men were ten to twenty years older than me, and most of them hailed from the torrid state of Queensland, which is famous for spawning in its hot and haggard bush the most cantakerous and belligerent of Australians. To tell the truth, I'm not so sure that I'd enjoy their company now. But back then, under those grim circumstances, I wouldn't have wanted to be with anyone else.

Let me also make it clear that there was no glad-handing when I walked into camp—that's not their style either—but I was made to feel that I belonged. The Aussies adopted me, called me Kid, or Yank, or Dougo, and they treated me leniently in regard to their multiple taboos. The men who liked me and looked out for me seemed to think of me as their younger brother, or, in some cases, as their son. These men seemed to recognize that I was still growing—that my body needed more food than a full-grown man's, if I was to survive—and the server at mealtime would invariably scoop up the few grains of rice sticking to the side of the pot and give them to me. That's why I credit the Aussies with getting me through, and that's why I came to love and respect them more than I could ever hope to express. And that's also why, in the future, I'm including myself when I refer to them; "we" means me and the Aussies, and not the Brits.

Which is not to suggest that every single Australian in camp accepted me into the fold; naturally, some of them resented the special treatment I received, and I suppose they had every right to feel that way. Indeed, growing up in and trying to integrate into a strange culture was the root cause of all my non-medical problems at the Hotel Tacloban. To begin with, coming from such a demanding environment, the average Australian male had already passed through adolescence and entered adulthood by the time he was my age, and he fully expected me to behave like a man. But I wasn't a man, and I never really understood what was going on. Hell, it took six months before I could follow a normal conversation, and I was always lost when the Aussies reminisced about things back home in Australia (things like billabongs and jumbucks, etc.) which I could make no reference to in my own experience. And rather than risk appearing as stupid and childish as I felt inside, my reaction was never to question or complain, and to work as hard as (if not harder than) anyone else. I tried to win their respect on that basis. What's more, I refused to use their lingo, even after I came to understand it completely, and in every respect I endeavored to remain exactly what I was—the Kid, the Yank. Consequently, no matter what I said or did, I felt that I was under constant scrutiny—that I was forever being judged on how well I stood up to the pressures heaped upon us by the Major and the Japanese. No matter where I was in camp the American flag was flying over my head. I may have gone overboard at times, asserting my identity as an American soldier, but that independent posture served me well, and in the end the Aussies called me landsman.

Lest I've given the wrong impression, let me assure you that even a mob of untamed Australian soldiers needs someone to hold them together, and for us that man was Lieutenant Gerard Duffy, the first person to greet me at the Hotel Tacloban. Despite the fact that Major Cumyns of the English Army was the ranking POW officer, it was Duff, for all practical intents and purposes, who was our one and only leader. I can testify to that on the basis of my own experience, for whereas the Major (having no interest in an insignificant American enlisted man) had refused to even acknowledge my presence, Duff had immediately taken me under his wing, instantly winning my loyalty.

Gerard Duffy came from the urbane, sophisticated city of Melbourne, which is located at the extreme southern tip of Australia. (Notably, out of a total population of seven million in 1940, one million Aussies called that teeming metropolis home.) One of only a handful of men in camp who had been to college, Duff had been studying law at the time of the call-up, had enlisted straight off, and, in view of his higher education, had been made an officer—a role he sometimes felt uncomfortable with. Nevertheless, he was determined to carry out his duty, to survive, and to return to Melbourne to follow (as a barrister) in both his father's and his grandfather's professional footsteps. Tall and slim, fair-haired and freckled, Duff was very Irish looking. And he was young, too—at twenty-five, he was one of the youngest men in camp.

Duff's biggest problem was a severe head wound he had received just prior to his capture; a hunk of steel had lodged in the left side of his skull, about an inch above and behind the ear, causing him chronic, agonizing fits which left him incapacitated fifty percent of the time. It was common knowledge that head wounds as bad as Duff's rarely if ever got better—that the terrible migraine-sized headaches only persisted and got worse—but Duff never complained. When the problem acted up, he disappeared into his hut for a few days and no one, not even his hutmates, Jerry and Carroll (the

51

other two Australian officers), were allowed inside until it had passed. When it was over, when he finally emerged from hiding, his eyes inevitably would be ringed by huge black circles and he would have the look of a man who had just returned from a trip to hell. But Duff never bored anyone with his personal problems, which is one of the many reasons why he was placed on a pedestal by his countrymen. Duff was a soldier's soldier—the rare type of man who could maintain a semblance of order among a crew of hostile Australian roughnecks trapped in a disgusting Japanese POW camp.

Duff was a natural-born leader—one in a million—the only officer in camp who had everything under control. And yet he did not look like or act like a disciplined soldier, let alone an officer, and therein lay the secret of his success. On the surface Duff was one among equals, but underneath the good-old-boy facade lurked an extraordinarily shrewd officer who, having been with his men for nearly two years (first in Libya where they had mixed it up with the "Eye-ties," then later in Borneo where they were captured), knew each one of them inside-out. He knew who the ringleaders were, who the loud-mouths were, who he could reason with, who he could talk down, and he knew which men would only understand violence. Although he preferred to rely on finesee to handle sticky situations and to command respect, if he gave an order to a trouble-maker, and if the guy did not respond immediately, Duff would simply haul off and bust him on the chops, right in front of everyone. And yet no one ever saluted him or called him sir; it was, "Hey, Duff!" and that was it.

A thoroughly remarkable man with many outstanding leadership qualities, Duff moved about the prison yard with an easy equanimity that inspired confidence. He never played favorites and never sloughed off responsibilities or ordered anyone to do anything he was not physically capable of doing himself. He was a real cool cat who could stare down anybody in camp and everyone (including the Major, with whom he was constantly at odds, although the subject of their rivalry was never mentioned in public) was intimidated by him. The bottom line about Duff was this: he did not stand on much formality, but he didn't take any shit.

Chapter Seven

Eight men were quartered in my hut when I arrived at the Hotel Tacloban; each one deserves a brief portrayal.

Pip Johnson, at forty-two, was the oldest as well as the raunchiest man in camp. Short and bandy-legged, sporting leathery skin and a long white beard, Pip also boasted the filthiest vocabulary, a habit he'd acquired while sheepshearing in the bush. By its very nature sheepshearing dulls a man's finer sensibilities, and it was the only work Pip had ever known. Paid by the number of sheep he sheared, Pip stood in one spot all day long, wearing hip boots and a thick leather apron, shearing away as fast as he could, gradually becoming inured to the volumes of sheep piss and sheep shit that mounted around him. His conversation, which I found repulsive, reflected his experience and focused on certain unmentionable biological similarities between ewes and women. It would be a gross understatement to say that Pip's personal habits were slightly too uninhibited for my tastes. Rounding out his rather crude character, Pip was an incessant, noxious farter, and needless to say, I slept as far away from him and his durable odor as I could.

Harry Barnsworth hailed from a small town in Queensland where he operated a semi-legitimate mercantile agency, collecting and furnishing information to his straight customers about the financial standing, credit rating, etc., of individuals, firms and corporations. Harry also acted as a loan shark and engaged in a variety of shady deals in order to satisfy his crooked clientele. As is so often true of Aussies, his father and grandfather had been in the same business. Harry was in his late twenties, was intelligent, possessed average good looks, and was the only circumsized Aussie I ever saw, which led me to believe he may have been Jewish.

Ray Barnes, who everyone called Carney, was hard and mean and tough as nails. Somewhere in his mid-thirties, Ray had worked as a roustabout in carnivals all over Australia. He was a massive man, well over six feet tall, who never demonstrated pain or concern, even though he had ugly running sores (the result of beriberi) covering his back. He was one of the few men in camp who sustained an aversion to me, until, as in any close-knit family, the bond between us grew sufficiently strong to replace his initial mistrust.

Jerry "Jocko" Ferris was not to be trusted. A compulsive scavenger and thief whom we would periodically catch stealing little bits of rice, or matches, or cigarettes, Jocko was the one Aussie in camp to be shunned by his countrymen, and he may have been an informer. If a group of guys were standing around shooting the breeze and Jocko came along, they'd disperse. Even Pip avoided him. Jocko was also in his mid-thirties.

Larry Whitlam was a laid-back farmer from Queensland, very shy, very retiring, not quite thirty years old. He had flaming red hair and freckles, and he was so skinny that he looked consumptive. Larry's background was uniquely Australian: his granddad had been a factory worker in London until he was convicted of stealing three or four loaves of bread, which was a capital offense in merry-old England at the time. However, because he wasn't a professional thief (just a poor desperate man) he was given a light sentence, relatively speaking—he was exiled to Australia where he was to pay his debt to society as an indentured farmer. Thanks to the merciful English judicial system, his wife and children were permitted to follow him several years later. Larry's grandfather worked for a squatter (an Australian ex-convict who'd done his time and subsequently acquired land of his own) for twenty years before he too was released from bondage and given a piece of land and some sheep of his own. By the time the Second World War erupted, the family farm had grown into a fairly good-sized spread. Incidentally, Larry's father fought at Gallipoli.

I liked Larry a lot, although we had little to do with one another. He was extremely guarded about his innermost feelings, as well as in choosing his words, but he was honest and brave and he always treated me well. His one fault was a quick temper, and at one point he flew into Jocko (who was rummaging around Larry's pad without his permission), grabbed him by the throat and swore, "I'll do you this time, you bloody bastard," and probably would have, if Travis hadn't pulled him off. Just for the record, Duff moved Jocko out of the hut immediately thereafter.

Bossy Petersen, a Swedish-Australian and thus an anomaly of sorts, was one of the many men in camp whose real name I never learned—it would have been a breach of Australian etiquette to have asked. Bossy was big and blonde and he'd earned his tag, obviously, from always telling everyone what to do. He never changed. Before the war, Bossy had been employed on a tugboat in Botany Bay.

As you've undoubtedly noticed, most Aussies had been christened with a bushname—a nickname based on occupation or personality or, more likely, some prominent physical defect. The names were endless and colorful—we had a Honker, a Sheep Dip, a Bucko, a Scratch and a Snotty, just to mention a few.

Justin "Jassy" Colby was a very popular fellow and a good friend of mine. About twenty-seven, tall, dark-haired and strikingly handsome, he was the prototype of the swashbuckling Australian male. A devout iconoclast, Jassy had a wonderful sense of humor and a big smile full of good teeth—a rarity among backwoods Australians. Jassy had been a bit of a scoundrel with the ladies, too, and his forte was in entertaining the troops for hours on end with explicit tales of sexual delight. For all their tough talk you'd have thought the Australians were all naive virgins, the way they sat around drooling, their tongues hanging out, listening eagerly while Jassy spun his licentious, pornographic yarns.

And yet, once you get to know the Aussies, it's easy to

understand why they acted that way. You see, most Australian soldiers, in 1942, did not have strong family ties; I'd estimate that less than ten percent of the men at the Hotel Tacloban were married, and even those with fiancees, like Duff, were a distinct, misunderstood minority. Why? Well, to begin with, the man to woman ratio in the northern hinterlands of Australia was a staggering twenty to one—a fact of life which, by forcing the bushmen to sublimate their unsatisfied sexual needs, undoubtedly reinforced their masochistic urge for hard physical labor. In any case, the typical Australian bushman suffered from an abundant lack of opportunity, and women, who were thoroughly misunderstood, were either venerated as other-worldly goddesses, or else viewed as mere instruments of pleasure. Summing up the prevailing sentiment in camp, Cracker McKevitt (our resident sage) professed that getting married and raising a family was strictly an occupation for "the skirts."

Adding to the average Australian's profound ignorance of womankind was the total lack of informative discussion initiated by the few married men, for whom silence was the easiest way to deal with separation from wife and children, and among whose ranks the subject was taboo. Interestingly enough, it was also forbidden to speak about past combat experiences—there was no point in boring others with your own bad memories—and pining for fallen comrades, as well as for family at home, was something done in private. Of course no self-respecting Aussie would ever express or admit to having intimate feelings for, or suggest in any way that he was dependent on another man. Such things were tacitly known, if they were known at all, and under the circumstances that approach worked out for the best.

The eighth man in our hut, Travis MacNaughton, had emigrated to Australia as a young boy from one of the Shetland Islands, where, appropriately, his father made his living raising Shetland ponies. It was Travis's trade, too. He was short, only five feet five inches tall, but he was big-boned and muscular, and he was the most fearless son-of-a-bitch I'd ever met in my life. Although Aussies usually prefer large, menacing men as their leaders, Travis, who was an expert at handling big, dumb powerful animals, had the well-deserved reputation as the most level-headed, most respected man (officer or EM) in camp. When Travis spoke, which was seldom, everyone listened—especially Duff. I never once heard Duff say "No" to Travis, or contradict anything he said. But more importantly, no one ever dared to question Travis's integrity; when everything was falling apart, Travis was the *only* man in camp that everyone, Brit as well as Aussie, felt comfortable with doling out the rice. Travis's word was law. He was sole judge and jury in all disputes, territorial or otherwise, at the Hotel Tacloban.

Travis MacNaughton was a man of high principles, a reluctant NCO who adamantly refused the battlefield commissions he was repeatedly offered, a man totally unto himself who harbored deep suspicions about professional soldiers or anyone else who profited from war. Travis was my hero. Having emigrated to Australia as an adolescent, he was the only man in camp beside Duff who was aware of the problems I was having adjusting to Australian culture and speech, and he took out the time to explain those things to me. And he was my guardian, too. When Carney decided to take my spot in the hut (which, unlike his, was out of the rain), Travis stood in between us and said, "There'll be non o' tha' in this hoot, mon," and that was the end of it. Thanks to Travis, I didn't have one fight with an Australian in all the time I was there. Travis was mid-thirtyish, one of the few married men in camp, the one man I was certain would survive intact; but he was typically Scottish, dour and withdrawn and, I regret to say, never as close to me as I would have liked.

Within our hut, Travis slept near the front entrance, his feet at my head. Jassy slept behind me, his head at my feet, then came Bossy, then Jocko. Larry's pad was opposite Travis's, then came Harry, Carney and Pip.

Like the Australians themselves, each hut at the Hotel Tacloban had its own distinct personality. One, for instance, leaned more toward the political. Another one was more quarrelsome. Another hut housed homosexuals. Taking into ac-

57

count the universal need to conserve energy (a dominant fact of life which held everyone's natural impulse "to do" firmly in check), the one characteristic which distinguished our hut from all the others was our apparent lack of motivation. Here again it was Travis who set the pace. Following his example, the rest of us consciously maintained a very low profile, rarely appropriating cigarettes or rice wine, rarely involving ourselves overtly in the politics or the management of the camp. Which, along with the fact of Travis' presence, may well explain why our hut held together better than most.

Like most men in camp I spent seventy-five percent of my time with the members of my hut, but it was important to form relationships outside the home, in order to reduce domestic tension, and I did make an effort to meet other men. By far the most interesting hut, in my opinion, belonged to the Diggers, who, as the embodiment of Australian ideals of independence and masculinity, held an exhalted rank in the Aussie hierarchy. Let me explain why: although the generic term "Digger" is widely applied to Australian soldiers in general (the way Yank might be used to describe a Texan, God forbid), in its pure, unadulterated form the word "Digger" applies exclusively to prospectors—eccentric men who threw off the trappings and hypocrisies of civilization in exchange for the unfettered freedom of desert, sun, and wind. Like the legendary mountain men of American folklore—the Daniel Boones and Davy Crocketts—the Diggers staked their reputations on their recklessness (when they weren't baiting the Japanese guards they were doing time in the Doghouse), *and* on their ability as bullshit artists. Fooling an audience into believing the most preposterous, the most blatant of fictions, through an elaborate fabrication of plausible half-truths and downright deceptions, was a Digger's highest level of achievement. Much to the eternal gratification of their fellow Australians, the Diggers were consummate liars.

Chief spokesman for the Diggers, and a man whom I counted among my friends, was Cracker McKevitt, an Irish Republican emigré blessed with the gift of gab, who enchanted me for hours on end with dubious accounts of his exploits as a swagman and gold prospector in the rough and tumble Australian outback. According to Cracker, shit and two made eight and the bloody Brits were directly responsible for all the world's woes.

Characteristically, Cracker had someone managed to smuggle a cribbage board and a deck of playing cards into camp— a feat of daring and ingenuity which further elevated him in my innocent eyes. Indeed, between his penchant for fairytales and my affection for games of chance, cribbage quickly became my favorite pastime at the Hotel Tacloban, and I spent most of my leisure hours in Cracker's hut pushing pegs. Not only was it a good way to kill time, but it was a good way to socialize.

In the final analysis, though, most socializing remained on a purely superficial level, and all in all there was a tendency *not* to form deep emotional attachments. The personnel within the small cliques which *did* form for companionship, for sharing cigarettes and for wiling away the endless, empty hours, was constantly changing and reforming due to the inevitable falling outs. By keeping the community homogenous, however, that fluidity worked to our collective advantage.

In regard to the friction between the Aussies (led by Duff) and the Brits (led by the Major), there was no hope of integration. It was the Hatfields versus the McCoys. Tension between the two feuding families was rife, and even though I was just an asshole kid, I could see at a glance that they were heading on a collision course. But more of that later on.

Chapter Eight

First thing every morning, the Japanese guards made the ranking British and Australian NCOs muster everyone in camp for morning roll call. Breakfast, which the Aussies called "morning," came next and consisted of rice boiled in a big black cast-iron cauldron kept beneath a portable thatch lean-to. Each man was allotted one wooden bowl, about five inches across and two inches deep, and some men had wooden spoons, but most of us made do with our fingers. During the first phase of our incarceration, each man received a level bowl of rice in the morning and another in late afternoon, with the Japanese guards doling it out in bulk to the British junior officers, with us (the enlisted men) preparing it ourselves on a rotating basis. In the beginning, two Japanese guards would oversee the distribution, but after a few months they lost interest and left the problem of equal portions for us to solve on our own. Which wasn't all that hard, actually; the most effective regulatory mechanism of all was at work—everyone watched everyone else like a hawk. The entire camp rose at sunrise like one big family, without reveille, without hestitation, without confusion. No one ever had to be called to "morning," you simply *had* to have the food.

At no time did the Japanese receive supplies from their own military command; whatever provisions *they* had, they'd confiscated from local Filipino farmers in exchange for counterfeit pesos. During the first phase, which was prior to the US Naval blockade of the Philippines, we occasionally came across a scrap of chicken or a fish head or fish tail floating in our starchy gruel, but those occasional pieces of fish or chicken were present in such small quantity that they only added flavor to the mush, never any nutritional value. And of course the Japanese, due to their smaller bodies, required a lot less food than we Caucasians, although as part of our punishment we were forced to subsist on substantially less; at night we went to bed so hungry that we couldn't sleep. But eventually we learned to live with a gnawing pain in our stomachs, and our stomachs themselves shrank to a point where eating was an issue only in so far as it was the source of strength that enabled us to carry on from day to day. In other words, we didn't look forward to eating, we ate automatically, simply to hold body and soul together. Incidentally, the Major and the British junior officers, who never looked under-fed, ate much better than we did.

Drinking water was drawn twice each day from a spigot alongside the Japanese barracks—always the bare minimum, never any for washing. As a result, our mess was a mobile home for disease-spreading flies, a medical problem we tried to manage, unsuccessfully, by moving it regularly from one location in camp to another. We had the same problem with our latrines, and we applied the same solution, with the same conspicuous lack of results, to the problem of human waste disposal. When it was our hut's turn to dig new slit trenches, Sergeant Donaldson or one of the other NCOs would stick his head inside and simply say, "Time to move, lads," which was our cue to fetch picks and shovels from the Japanese barracks and to cover over the old hole with dirt from the new.

Aside from missing decent food and medicine, we missed soap (there wasn't a single bar in camp, ever) and water for washing most of all. Rain served as our principle means of keeping clean, and whenever there was a good shower a crowd of naked filthy men would step outside to bathe, not unaware of the indignity. Starting at the top with their heads and shoulders, using their hands to scrub away the layers of dirt and grime, they worked their way down to their feet. But it was a losing battle and it just got harder and harder to sustain our health because of the water shortage. We didn't even have enough to clean the bowls we ate from. So, acting out of desperation, Duff, who became a fanatic about sanitation, ordered us to throw our bowls into the pot of boiling water. Which was a good idea except that some of the men went overboard and boiled their shorts, (which had a tendency to reek from dysentery discharge and chronic diarrhea) and that was a big mistake—the shorts only fell apart sooner as a result, and some of those fellows wound up walking around bare-ass naked or wearing loincloths made out of rags.

In terms of apparel, not one of the POWs wore a shirt, except the Major, and no one including the Major wore long pants. Both the Brits and the Aussies had come to camp outfitted in traditional English Army shorts, the baggy, khaki kind that hung down nearly to the knees. Being somewhat fashion conscious, I conformed to the popular style and cut my GI pants off at the same hemline.

Lack of water was also the principle cause of dysentery; next to malaria, the chronic diarrhea symptomatic of dysentery was our gravest health related problem in camp, causing men literally to shit their lives away. We had no toilet paper (one hand was reserved for wiping, the other was strictly for eating) and of course there was no way to help the men in the sick hut to keep clean, and they just languished in their own excrement. Only the Major received extra water for washing, but there weren't any razor blades in camp, so even he couldn't shave. When their beards grew too heavy for comfort (a problem I didn't have, because I didn't grow whiskers), the men would chomp them down with the one pair of dull scissors we did have. Within a year everyone had shoulder-length hair, which was tied back in braids or ponytails.

The shoes I'd been wearing when I was captured fell apart within six months and thereafter I walked around barefooted like everyone else, which was another problem of major proportions. There was no antiseptic or iodine to soothe the festering sores and blisters that made walking such a painful ordeal, and it took months before my feet toughened up and developed calluses. It was especially hard on our feet when they sent us out to work on Highway 1, and it was equally bad during the seasonal monsoons, which lasted from late August through November, and which I'd walked into upon my arrival in camp. "The wets," as the Aussies called the monsoons, made everything slimy. The mats we slept on, the bamboo and thatch in our huts, our clothes, even the skin on our feet was coated with a disgusting film of mold and mildew.

It was incredibly humid during "the wets," the air was saturated with microscopic, disease-carrying organisms, and we always felt chilled, and respiratory ailments flourished. "The wets are with us," the Aussies would say, then sigh, and you knew it was the start of a bad time.

Basically, the Hotel Tacloban was a slave-labor camp where short periods of idleness and boredom were punctuated by long stretches of arduous, enervating work. The eighty to ninety men who were physically capable of reporting for work details when I arrived in camp received their orders each morning from our NCOs, via the British junior officers, that it was time to "do a day." We'd line up after breakfast, dopey from fever and fatigue, Brits in the front ranks, then shuffle off to work on the road or on the docks in Tacloban. Unlike the cheerful crew pictured in "The Bridge On The River Kwai," no one was whistling or marching in step; like the stone-roller, Sisyphus, we found no satisfaction in our futile, forced labor. It was hatred of the Japanese, and that alone, which enabled us to push Highway 1 back and forth across the steaming plain.

Organization of work details had been assigned to the Major by Captain Yoshishito, but even the mere thought of manual labor was beneath his station, so the Major (who was never present at work) left the application of his commands in that respect to his underlings. Consequently, work details were supervised by the British junior officers under the watchful eye of our sadistic Japanese guards, who answered to no one. To make their wishes known the guards used a combination of graphic gestures, gibberish and wild gesticulations; when those things failed to get across their meaning, they resorted to violence. Men who didn't work hard enough to suit the guards were beaten senseless, even if they were wracked by malaria and dysentery, and it was a daily occurrence for sick men to collapse from exhaustion and heat prostration.

Within the chain of command at the Hotel Tacloban, the Japanese guards directed the Brits, and the Brits divvied up the chores, but neither the Brits nor the Japanese guards could persuade the Aussies (who did most of the work) to toil diligently unless Duff was there to relay their orders. He may never have lifted a shovel, but Duff worked as hard as anyone else. Administering to those who collapsed, pulling them under any available shade, distributing water fairly and defusing potentially explosive situations, Duff held the work crews together, simply because he was there. As the Japanese and the Brits were both well aware, after much trial and error, without Duff, nothing would have been accomplished.

For the most part work was limited to road repair, although on occasion we were sent to Tacloban to sink pilings for new docks or to unload Japanese freighters. (Although work on the road was much harder, I preferred it to working in Tacloban—a handful of avidly anti-Anglo Filipinos liked to throw insults, garbage, even stones at us while we were on the docks, and I hated being humiliated.) Work on the cowpath called Highway 1 proceeded in frenzied sprints—they'd work us hard for ten or twelve days in a row, then lay off for two or three while they located a qualified engineer in Tacloban to verify that the road was heading in the right direction. The only other time work would stop was when the Japanese ran out of the flat, heavy pieces of shale we used to widen and surface the road, and which we also used for installing culverts during the wets. Work periods generally lasted somewhere between eight and ten hours and were always conducted under the most hysterical of conditions, with the guards screaming and hollering at us the entire time, pushing us and shoving us but never gaining any time or distance for their efforts. We worked without shade or protective clothing under the searing sun until our backs and shoulders were charred chestnut brown, until we fainted from dehydration and heat prostration.

Things got progressively worse on the work details as time went on, with reeling men staggering down to the cowpath, propping themselves up on their picks and shovels, passing out cold after fifteen minutes in the sun. On some days more than half the men would collapse, becoming utterly useless to bemused Japanese guards more concerned with inflicting pain than in accomplishing work. Why the guards acted that way, I never knew, although I suppose it made them feel like men, or maybe it satisfied their apparent need to feel superior to us. Whatever the reason, it was senseless cruelty on their part, and there were instances when men would crack under the strain. The pattern was usually the same: the man would begin to foam at the mouth like a rabid dog, race around in circles, stop suddenly and stand perfectly still. Then, as if in the throes of an epileptic fit, his body would fly into grotesque contortions; a leg might kick out, or his head might snap back in a violent spasm, his eyes bulging horribly, or both arms might shoot straight up and stay there like steel ramrods. The man might jump up and spin around in mid-air, like he was trying to catch someone sneaking up behind him. But he wasn't. His movements were all involuntary, his mind an utter blank. At the end he'd fall on the ground, screaming and kicking and clawing at the earth, shoveling handfuls of dirt into his mouth. It was a pathetic sight, but there was nothing we could do, and even though most men recovered from such episodes, we did have four psychotic cases at the Hotel Ta-cloban—men who had to be restrained to keep them from harming themselves; men who were incapable of feeding or cleaning themselves; men who'd lost the will to live.

Despite the brutality of the Japanese guards, the worst struggle at work was among ourselves. We'd be strung out over an average of two hundred yards, with each man performing his individual task, either breaking up the ground with a pick, or raking, or shoveling, or lugging pieces of shale, or pulling the heavy roller we used to flatten out the sod, which was the hardest task of all—discipline and camaraderie vanished as everyone postured to avoid that job. The fight for water was equally vicious, with each man rushing to position himself as close as possible to one of the two or three pails of water interspaced along the line, with the strongest men using their muscle to guarantee themselves a drink. And naturally, what with Duff absent half the time, the British officers took full advantage of the situation, placing their own troops nearest to the water buckets and assigning their own men to the softest jobs (the British EMs got the rakes and we got the shovels and the roller). There were innumerable fights over water and work assignments; in fact these things were the principle cause of the hatred between the Brits and the Aussies, as well as being the main reason why the Aussies suffered so much more illness and death.

To the best of my ability I tried to occupy a central position in the on-going struggle on the road gang, with the one fight I did have occurring during my first week on it. Here's how it happened: buckets were filled once in the morning and lasted all day long. But it was torture to have to stand there and watch the water evaporate before your eyes and someone would always take a few extra gulps as the day wore down. Late one afternoon, as I moved to drink my allotted share, a British sergeant cut in front of me and polished off the pail. Everyone saw him do it, and I didn't stop to ask him why, I just slugged him. Once was enough. He didn't pursue it. But the incident was reported when we returned to camp, and I was brought before the Major for disciplinary action.

The fact that he never lifted a finger at work didn't prevent the Major from affecting a sanctimonious attitude concerning my indiscreet behavior on the road gang; in fact the man was so vain, so overbearing, that he deigned to speak directly to me, channeling his comments through Lieutenant Downey instead, who then forwarded them on to me as follows: the Major was terribly upset by my unruly actions and was afraid that I might prove to be a typical American trouble-maker; I had acted impetuously and with no regard for the general morale; I should have reported the incident to the Major through the proper channels; discipline was the Major's responsibility, not mine, and only *he* was entitled to mete out punishment; if I ever did anything like that again, he would see to it personally that I was court-martialed as soon as we were rescued; the facts of the incident were being recorded in "the Book," and I would deeply regret any further violations of camp decorum; dismissed.

But there was more to it than the Major was willing to acknowledge; I *had* to establish beyond any doubt that no one could steal my water without paying the price. In so far as that was crucial to my survival, I succeeded—no one ever attempted to take my water again. Nevertheless, I hadn't been in camp one week and already I was on the shitlist. Not only that, I hadn't been allowed to utter one word in my own defense, and I was mad. I was beginning to see what we were up against in the form of our Camp Commandant, Major R.L. Cumyns.

Chapter Nine

Major Roland Leeds Cumyns, who was in his early thirties, was a relatively young man to hold field rank in the English Army. He had soft green eyes, a slight build and a delicate complexion, dainty (almost effeminate) mannerisms he would have characterised as aristocratic, and an irritating, haughty accent which was noticably more pronounced than that of any other British soldier in camp. Everything about him indicated quite clearly that he had been "to the manor born."

Major Cumyns was the most arrogant, most conceited son-of-a-bitch I'd ever come across in my life; an impossible officer who was thoroughly convinced that God was an Englishman. Rooted in the ruling class, reared by private tutors and sent to one of the most prestigious public schools, the Major was also a graduate of the Royal Military Academy, Sandhurst. The English equivalent of West Point (only more deeply imbedded in the ancient, feudal, military caste system), RMA Sandhurst prefers to recruit the sons of English officers and NCOs, or, in some special cases, the sons of the landed gentry. "Gentleman Cadet" Cumyns, as graduates of Sandhurst are called, was one of the latter.

What type of man was the typical, pre-World War Two gentleman cadet? A well-mannered, well-connected chap who excelled at polo and cricket and the other essential field sports, the sort of fellow you could count on to know the difference between a port glass and a sherry glass. While training at "The Shop" (as Sandhurst is known to insiders—although The Closed Shop describes it more accurately), a gentleman cadet accepted as his birthright all the traditional advantages afforded the privileged few. For example, if need be, examination questions could be bought before tests, not only to ensure passing grades, but also to spare Sandhurst the unpleasantness of having to expel cheaters, as West Point must do periodically. According to Duff this time-honored practice

was employed with great success by many illustrious gentle-
men cadets, including, most notably, the English Prime Min-
ister serving at the time. But that's just a rumor, of course.
There is no denying, however, that the Major was a member
of *the* most influential fraternal club in the waning British
Empire, one which filled the majority of policy-making army
posts during World War Two. Like most Sandhurst alumni,
the Major assumed he was fit to command men at war strictly
on the basis of an inherited belief that the lower classes were
meant to serve the upper classes, and that the upper classes
were meant to lead.

As a graduate of Sandhurst, the Major was irrevocably committed to a military career, and from the very moment of his
immaculate matriculation he had been groomed for success.
Pampered, primped and preened, the Major wholeheartedly
believed that it was his manifest destiny to ascend to the
pinnacle of his profession, from whence he would come to
enjoy the adulation of his peers. Bred to be high-strung, he
had never been prepared for disappointment or defeat. "Failure?" as Queen Victoria is reputed to have said, "The possibility does not exist." Maybe not, when you're perched
upon a throne, but anything can happen in the real world,
and it did. The Major was captured by the enemy and the
sudden shock of having to sit out the war in a wretched
Japanese POW camp had utterly destroyed the man. Doomed
to obscurity, the only recognition he could expect to receive,
in the foreseeable future, would come from his own dutiful
troops, or from the Japanese Camp Commandant, Captain
Yoshishito, with whom he had immediately ingratiated himself. The Major could certainly expect no respect from the
Australians, who recognized him solely for the mortal threat
he posed; to them he represented the hollow self-righteous-
ness of the bombastic British Empire, and nothing more. And,
naturally, my alliance with the Australians made me just one
more rebel to be viewed, from the Major's vantage point,
with utter contempt.

The Major took every opportunity to attend to his own
creature comforts while flaunting his disdain for the plight of
the Australians. Illustrative of his flagrant disregard for our

suffering was his utilization of his prerogative, as a field officer
in the English Army, to employ the services of a personal
lackey, one Corporal Trimbly; an arrangement which might
not have been as aggravating as it was, if it hadn't been for
the fact that Corporal Trimbly relished his subservience.
Trimbly understood the perquisites and obligations accom-
panying his role, and he fully accepted and supported the
caste system which weighed so heavily on the rest of us. In
return for shining his master's shoes, for cleaning his clothes,
for trimming his beard and for clipping his fingernails, for
existing at the Major's beck and call and for performing all
the functions of a personal valet, Corporal Trimbly knew
more, and ate more, than the other enlisted men. But even
more importantly, when the cannonballs were flying, Corporal Trimbly and those of his ilk were snuggled safely in a
rear area picking lint off their masters' uniforms. Personal
lackeys like Trimbly are usually not young men, and some
of them go so far as to follow their commanding officer into
retirement, with the English Army footing the bill.

I'd always admired the British, and from what I'd seen in
newsreels back home in Pleasantville they deserved our ad-
miration, if for no other reason but for the polite manner in
which they withstood those horrible German air-raids. Terror
bombing it was called, and some sections of London were
razed beyond recognition. I recalled breath-taking scenes of
total devastation; bomb craters filled the streets and brick
buildings had been reduced to marred foundations, piles of
smouldering rubble, and heaps of shattered glass. And yet the
Londoners themselves were carved in stone, honed by ad-
versity to the peak of resolution. An air of togetherness, of,
"We've got to see it through," pervaded that ravaged city and
gave it dignity. Although there must have been people who
were emotionally destroyed, I can only recall seeing people
responding to that nightmare with cheerful determination,
with a stiff upper lip and a firmly set jaw. You'd have thought
they were winning the war.

In London, an air-raid was business as usual; they toasted
Churchill, tossed down their drinks, then strolled casually to
the Underground, their combination subway system and bomb

shelter. Some came equipped with blankets and snacks, and soon they were playing card games, chatting about football or the weather, all in all making it rather homey down there in the dark gloomy recesses. And then, as the rumble and thunder of detonating bombs grew louder and closer, the Brits would begin to sing "Rule Britannia," "The Siegfried Line," and other patriotic songs in gleeful defiance of Jerry and the hellish world he was creating above. Afterwards, when it was over, when the horn blew the All Clear, they emerged from hiding to dig out the unexploded bombs, to put out the fires, to care for the wounded, and to bury the dead. But they never showed any signs of quitting.

Perhaps it was their innate sense of superiority which pulled the English through the dark days of 1940 and 1941, when their island fortress was besieged by the Luftwaffe, when they were utterly alone, with their backs to the wall. Maybe their grace under such unheard of pressure excuses their condescending attitude toward the rest of humanity. For instance, their good-natured disapproval of the Yanks, as "Over paid, over sexed, and over here." Or their opinion that the Scandinavians are a dispossessed and destitute race; or that the Scots are a pack of kilted freebooters; or that the Irish are uninteresting, unintelligent, and ungovernable; or that the Australians are hopeless prodigals. Perhaps one must experience their class and race prejudice first-hand before one can truly appreciate the British.

Captain Yoshishito (whose motto was "divide and conquer") had made the Major personally responsible for maintaining discipline among prisoners; if there were any violations of the rules, the Major was expected to report the guilty man for punishment, a course of action which usually led to a stint in the Doghouse, a beating by the guards, and sometimes worse. The Japanese allowed the British to exercise complete control over the Aussies, and this was an arrangement which pleased the Major immensely. And he went about doing it (in true British military fashion) in a manner far and above that which was necessary, at times reporting men who'd committed only petty misdemeanors. Of course, outside of re-

71

porting us to the Japanese there was actually very little he *could* do; knowing that any decrease in our meager rations would cause a riot, the Major, to his credit, never used food as a tool of punishment. Latrine duty and mess duty were the usual penalties handed out for minor crimes (like fighting or laziness or failing to salute) which were not reported to the Japanese.

Ultimately, though, the weapon which the Major used most effectively—the one which caused the greatest concern—was The Book, in which he kept a record of every offense, and who had committed it, for reckoning after our release. Not knowing how he had embellished his accounts in it troubled us deeply, and, like the sword of Damocles, The Book hung over our heads, reminding those of us on its pages that our problems weren't necessarily over when we were rescued. It was blackmail, pure and simple.

We felt that the Major, by demanding our complete submission, was aiding and abetting the enemy, and we felt that he was deliberately compounding the pressures on us rather than taking steps to reduce them. He wanted us to think that he was doing us a favor by collaborating with Captain Yoshishito, but we knew better; his complicity was motivated, in fact, by fear he could not conceal. It was obvious to everyone that our lovely Major had willingly sold us out for assurances of safety and comfort, and knowing that did more than demoralize and enrage us, it crippled us. It was like being stabbed in the back.

The bastard even went so far as to give his word of honor that there would be no escapes. (If he hadn't given his word, he would have been treated as badly as the rest of us, perish the thought.) What's more, just to make sure that *we* honored his agreement with the Japanese, the Major prowled the camp at night like a junkyard dog, checking each and every hut at unpredictable hours ranging from dusk until dawn. Furthermore, the Major *insisted* that every man take a solemn oath *not* to escape (even though it was our sworn duty to try) and he cold-bloodedly informed us that any man who tried, and who was caught, could expect punishment in traditional Japanese form—death by decapitation. He didn't understand that more than food or water or medicine or rest, we craved our freedom. But it was useless to argue with the Major. So, in an effort to avoid a futile confrontation over the issue, one by one we promised, with our fingers crossed behind our backs, that we would never try to escape. Meanwhile, the hatred toward him smouldered beneath a facade of compliance.

What really ignited the hatred toward the Major was his insane demand that any man suffering from malaria, which seventy-five percent of us had, must report for work if he wasn't having chills, or if his fever, whether rising or falling, was not at its peak. Over time this order became a virtual death sentence for many men, especially as we received shorter and shorter rations and as our ability to withstand the parasite that had a hold on our bodies decreased. Not only did he require that men with malaria report to work, but anyone who was ambulatory, even if wracked by dysentery, was also expected to "do a day." And there were instances when he refused to follow his own guidelines when determining who was fit to work. He'd walk from hut to hut, sending in his lieutenants to examine our sick, sometimes even pulling men out of the sick hut and calling them malingerers. Of course he never actually touched anyone who was ill, for fear of contaminating himself; rather, he stood outside, asked probing questions, then sent in one of his hatchetmen to do the dirty work.

It was utterly degrading, but we had no means of contesting his medical pronouncements. Because we had no thermometer, we were relegated to judging a man's fitness to work strictly on the basis of his physical appearance, which was obviously an unreliable method. Case in point: the initial phase of malaria shows profuse sweating and a rapid rise in temperature, and the effects of dehydration are clearly visible at this point; the man's lips are cracked and white and crimson blotches break out all over his face and neck. The critical stage comes next, when the sweating stops, at which point the temperature can either rise or fall. Chills signal a falling temperature, but if the temperature began to rise, and there was always a chance that it might, there was no telling how high it might go, and a man could quite literally burn-up inside and expire. It was impossible to predict what would happen next, or to what degree, but such considerations mattered little to our fine Major, who dispassionately ordered our most serious malaria cases off to work, often on the basis of a cursory glance.

Somewhere along the line the Major's mind had snapped and, in order to justify his criminal actions, he became obsessed with expounding upon the virtues of "putting on a good show," of turning out as many men each day as was super-humanly possible. He began to rant and rave about malingerers—exhortations which were as transparent as they were irrational—and he willingly forfeited the lives of men he was, according to all military rules and traditions, duty bound to protect, just to meet his quotas, just so he could remain in Captain Yoshishito's good graces. But we were powerless to alter the situation, and after awhile it didn't bother us that the Major never looked underfed, or that his shorts were always clean and neatly creased, or that he expected sick men to work before himself. To our way of thinking he wasn't one of us anyway. Hell, he wasn't even a soldier.

Indeed, our primary, if not sole, value to the Japanese, and thus to the Major, was as slave-laborers who produced more than what was minimally required to sustain our wretched existence. Only then were we worth our keep. We were aware of that fact, painfully so, and like workers on a slow-down strike in a factory, we sought to do as little work as possible. We also felt that it was our duty to screw up the equipment whenever we got the chance, as a means of resisting the enemy and of preserving our self-respect. But these tactics also pitted us against the Major, who insisted that we return our tools in good condition at the end of each work period, and who professed, straight-faced, that a "job well-done" was good for morale as well as a credit to the aptitude of the British soldier.

Needless to say, the Aussies didn't think of themselves as British soldiers, anymore than I did, and they wouldn't have cooperated with the hated Japanese in any case. They knew they were a commodity the Major traded to Captain Yoshishito simply to assure his own continued comfort and safety. In no way did he serve as our agent; he was our exploiter and tormentor, that's all.

Chapter Ten

Trouble at the Hotel Tacloban revolved around the Major, the perverse love-hate relationship he had with his troops, and the tension that relationship produced between the Brits and the Aussies, which at first seemed very strange to me. I couldn't understand why the two supposed allies mistrusted one another, or why they were constantly at one another's throats—even Travis hated the Brits. But the sad fact of the matter was this: the Brits, who were all career soldiers who respected and feared the Major and made a show of kissing his ass, actually felt threatened by the recalcitrant Aussies, none of whom had any intentions of making a career out of the military, or of playing by its rules.

I suppose it's a cultural foible with the English (certainly any nation that nurtures and glorifies a royal family, at huge public expense, necessarily develops an unnatural devotion to figures of authority), but it was embarrassing to watch the Brits grovel at the Major's feet. For their part the Aussies looked down upon the Brits with disgust and wondered how any self-respecting man, especially a soldier, could allow himself to accept such a demeaning, subservient role. No Aussie in his right mind would ever play the toy soldier, or yield to someone regardless of his merits. Aussies rendered their loyalty to individuals of proven worth, not to abstracts like office or rank.

Ironically, although outnumbered by the Aussies three to one, the Brits monopolized the administration of the camp. Because they were so well organized, they had effectively segregated themselves (physically and socially) and they constantly imposed their will upon the anarchistic Australians. Those same qualities which the Aussies found so unmanly enabled the British to cooperate with one another, to work together as a unit, and thus to manage the affairs of the camp to the never-ending detriment of the Australians. And, naturally, the Brits looked down on the Aussies as insubordinate, uncouth heathens one grade *below* monkeys in a zoo, commenting freely on the rough-and-ready life-style the Aussies were accustomed to, focusing their criticism on how infrequently the Aussies bathed, or on the total lack of meaningful conversation discoverable in Australian social circles. ("Hey there, mate," and a shove on the shoulder *was* about the extent of it.) The Aussies got even by beating on the Brits, or, when that wasn't possible, by beating on themselves.

Unquestionably, the Australians were oriented more toward the physical than the cerebral, a condition which overlapped into their unique brand of humor. Humor which, relying more on slapstick than on wit, took some getting used to. For instance, we all had lice in our hair, and just for a laugh an Aussie would rub his hand in his crotch, then playfully put a handful of the pesty little critters on another man's head. Or if someone was squatting over the slit-trench (a painful experience due to the convulsions resulting from dysentery), it was not unusual for some passing Aussie to stop, say, "Hi there, mate" then push the guy backwards into the slop. *That* was considered a hilarious joke, although the butt of such a joke would have to scrub down with sand and sleep outside his hut until the next good rain came along and washed his stink away.

Distinguishing between an insult and a joke was, at times, quite a challenge. On more than one occasion I watched while one Aussie flipped another Aussie's rice bowl out of his hands; then a group of them would stand around laughing while the poor fellow picked up the scattered grains. Unbelievable—I could never understand why something as serious as that wasn't cause for a fight, when minor misunderstandings or mistakes were.

Some Aussies were *too* damn physical, like Rodney Burgess, the camp gorilla and prime example of a man who overcompensated for his intellectual inadequacies by pushing around his excessive weight. If he's alive today, Rodney is undoubtedly residing in some Australian penitentiary; he was always beating up somebody, usually over nothing. He even looked the part. His face was a mess from countless fights—

ripped ears, broken teeth, crooked nose, scars galore—and yet, for some inexplicable reason, Rodney felt superior to everyone else, and he was the only man in the camp who refused to say "Hi" to me. But Australians admire bullies and, through a policy of brute strength and awkwardness, Rodney had assumed executive directorship of his hut.

Despite the fact that Rodney was twice as big and twice as strong as anyone else in camp, he was also (as bullies so often are) twice as easily confused; which brings me to the time several Australians were charged with the care of two goats the Japanese guards brought into camp. (This was during the first phase of our imprisonment, when we were still able to laugh.) Anyway, within a few days these Aussies (who had been farmers in civilian life) had trained the goats to deposit their goat feces in neat little piles wherever they wanted, and soon thereafter the goats were doing their duty behind Rodney's hut. The heap got higher and higher but Rodney never noticed; his hut was adjacent to the infirmary, where our worst dysentery cases were quarantined, and the odor issuing forth from it vastly overpowered all other smells. Eventually, when the pile reached conspicuous proportions, persons unknown stuck a sign in it which read, "Rodney shit here!" Because he couldn't read, Rodney was among the last to get the joke, and when he did find out, he was mortified.

Rodney spent the remainder of his time at The Hotel Tacloban, which was until we were rescued (the Rodneys of the world always seem to make it), investigating the crime, trying to discover who the culprit was. And although he never did solve the case, in one sense you could say that we did him a favor: you see, Rodney was never able to articulate exactly what it was that he was mad about, and this gave him something tangible to which he could attach his monumental wrath.

One last word about Rodney: usually when there was a fight between the men, Duff would send Jerry Simms to break it up. A swarthy, physically powerful man who had earned his commission in the field, Jerry would bull his way through, if he could. (Carroll Spaulding, Duff's other lieutenant, handled administrative problems; tall and prissy, always picking his nose, Carroll was described by Cracker as "putting on the skirts.") But Rodney was too much for Jerry to manage, and time and time again Duff had to step in personally to prevent Rodney from breaking someone into pieces. Duff's approach seldom varied; he's walk up to Rodney and say, as if he were addressing a man of great importance, "Now, Rod," (Duff never called him Rodney, which was the secret to his success), "go back to your hut, park your ass on your pad, and stay there until I say move."

Rodney would fume, but he'd do it. Even he was smart enough to know that anyone who laid a hand on Duff would have woken up dead the next morning. Even Rodney realized that Duff was indispensable—that Duff was the only person who could hold us together and pull us through. Us meaning the Aussies, that is.

The only time the Brits and Aussies were in any way unified (other than at funerals) was during our Sunday church services, which were held in front of a different hut each week, with a core group of about forty of us, including all officers, forming the permanent congregation. Enlisted men bound by a common faith patched up their differences on Sunday morning, and, like good Christians everywhere, returned to feuding on Sunday afternoon. Officers, however, were unable to bridge the cultural gap, even for thirty minutes, and the Major sat with his staff in the front row on one side, while Duff and Jerry and Carroll sat up front on the other side. I usually went with Travis.

These rag-tag affairs were one of the rare instances when, as a matter of democratic principle (specifically, majority rule), the Australian EMs took precedence over the proceedings (although fewer Aussies than Brits actually attended). Jeff Connelly, an Australian NCO and one of the better educated men in camp, was our unofficial pastor in this regard—an arrangement which satisfied everyone. Jeff was a natural for the role. He had a wonderful baritone voice, he knew most of the traditional Protestant hymns by heart, and he owned a Bible—the only other book in camp besides Duff's medical text. Nearly forty, bald and blind as a bat (he'd lost his glasses in combat), Jeff was seriously ill with malaria, beriberi and-

dysentery; but he was a devout Christian, a truly decent man, and recognized by everyone as such.

In sharp contrast to the Brits, who were Episcopalians to the man, there was really no such thing as an organized Australian religion, and Cracker once again summed up the prevailing Aussie opinion when he declared that only "the skirts" went to church. Most Aussies were either Irish Catholic renegades who'd escaped from under the yoke of the Roman Catholic Church and subsequently reverted to ancient Celtic paganism, or else, like myself, they were nonpracticing Protestants—although they all knew how to pray when it was absolutely necessary.

My own ambivalent feelings about religion were the result of having been shuffled from one relative to another in my youth. My mother and father divorced before I was one, and I was sent to live with my mother's parents, my Grandma and Grandpa Jensen; super-patriotic Danish immigrants who lived in Banksville, New York, straight-laced Congregationalists who saw God and the American flag as one and the same. When I was four, my mother remarried, retrieved me from my grandparents (whom I loved very much), and had me baptised and confirmed in the Pleasantville Methodist Church, where she was a prominent member. My mother, however, possessed a double-edged Puritanism; although unaffectionate, standoffish and a strict disciplinarian, she wanted other people to know that she had risqué ideas. As a child, I was never quite sure where I stood with her. My religious education was completed on my Aunt Gertie's dairy farm in Danbury, where I spent my summers as a youth. A fire and brimstone Baptist for whom one day of religion each week wasn't enough, Aunt Gertie saw to it that I learned the true meaning of sin at Wednesday night, "get-it-off-your-chest" revival meetings, that old-time religion.

Whatever positive feelings I'd ever had about religion died along with Bobby, who came from a very close-knit family and for whom faith in God was the center of his life. "Back home on the farm," he once said to me, "when I step out on the porch in the morning, everywhere I look I see God. I don't know why, exactly, but I suppose it's because farmers are dependent on the sun and the wind and the rain—on nature. They can't tell you why one year brings drought or flood, then the next year brings plenty, and I guess that dependence puts them closer to life's mystery." But I was too immature to understand, and Bobby's faith was a mystery to me and when he died, religion stopped making sense altogether. It wasn't until I'd been in the Hotel Tacloban for a while that I began to realize that I needed a source of strength beyond what I could provide for myself, and that's when I began to reform my beliefs.

The thing that really generated a lot of excitement at the Hotel Tacloban, arising spontaneously and involving both Aussies and Brits, was the advent of Christmas, 1942. For the first time since they'd arrived in camp six months earlier, a sense of brotherhood—of community—was evident between the two. Peace reigned. However, through sheer weight of numbers (a preponderance of good-will, so to speak) the Aussies seized control of the situation, and as soon as Captain Yoshishito had nodded his approval (via the Major), Jeff was delegated to organize a Christmas pageant play, which, as befitting any Australian production, was exclusively an enlisted man's affair. Although everyone was invited, all officers, Aussies too, were to remain spectators. Not that any of them were hurt. In fact the Major was very amused and predicted that the whole thing would fail miserably without his expert supervision. Damn him, he was almost right.

The moment Jeff set the machinery in motion, he was confronted by a dilemma of potentially disastrous proportions. None of the Aussies were familiar enough with the story of the Nativity, in the strict Biblical context, to organize the proceedings. Not only that, they had no props. What to do? The Aussies were in a quandary. The last thing they wanted was to see the Major gloating over their failure, but, on the other hand, national pride would not permit them to ask the British EMs for help. No one knew what to do. Until, in the selfless spirit of the Yuletide season, the Brits stepped forward with the following solution: the pageant play would remain ostensibly an Australian production, with Jeff as titular figurehead, but the management responsibilities would henceforth be handed over to the Brits, if no one objected. Everyone agreed, of course. It was no secret that the Brits had adjusted to prison life more successfully than the fractious Australians; unlike their provincial cousins the Brits worked together as a team, never allowing petty personal antagonisms to interfere in the smooth completion of their assigned tasks. Furthermore, they were Episcopalians one and all (otherwise known as Anglicans), they knew by heart the words to all the Christmas carols, and they were well versed in the appropriate sequence of events in the standard Christmas church service.

The Brits were also more adept at organizing material, and they were light-years more ingenious when it came to fashioning the necessary props. Somehow they managed to scrape together unused pieces of wood and bamboo lying around camp, and somehow they managed to construct a stage and a crib. Their actors, in the finest English dramatic tradition, were superlative; a fair-haired, fair-skinned Brit threw a piece of cloth over his head to play the part of the Virgin Mary, and a swarthy Brit with a long black beard played the role of Joseph. The Baby Jesus was represented by a stuffed shirt. I must admit, I was very impressed, and so were the Australians, although *they* never gave the Brits the satisfaction of admitting it.

Diplomacy between the Brits and Aussies was a highly refined art; whenever they wanted to iritate one another, without starting all-out war, they delivered formal letters. It was the one peaceful means of communication between them. Thus it came to pass, a few days before Christmas, that the Brits, in the interest of detente, sent a letter to Jeff indicating that they were unable to produce one integral prop; namely, the jackass. In essense, the letter was an appeal for help to the Australians, who, according to the Brits, were better suited to provide that part of the play. And just to add a dash of salt to the wound, the considerate Brits had also written down the words to "Silent Night," "O Little Town Of Bethlehem," and, "Hark! The Herald Angels Sing," on fragile pieces of brown rice paper, with a note attached which said something to the effect of: "Just in case you chaps have forgotten the words to these immortal hymns, as well as to ensure that this most holy ceremony is appropriately devout, we are providing you Australians with these humble English songbooks." I snuck into a corner and laughed until I cried.

The reaction among the Aussies was somewhat more sedate. Rodney, for one, was madder than hell; the last thing he wanted was to appear like the illiterate fool he was to the bloody Brits. Furious, he sought spiritual guidance from Jeff, who wisely counseled him not to fret, not to worry, just to "Hum along with the music, Rodney, or whistle." Which is precisely what he did.

The entire camp assembled in front of Jeff's hut on Christmas morning, officers up front on opposite sides, enlisted men behind (with some fraternizing), Japanese guards, armed and curious, everywhere. From their end of camp the British stage-hands proudly carried forth the platform, and the actors assumed their places. The pageant play began. Three wise men followed the star to the manger, gave presents to the Lord, then retired to the wings. Joseph and Mary beamed. Christmas carols followed. One of the Brits had come equipped with a pitch whistle, which he blew prior to each hymn so that everyone might sing on key, in harmony, in praise of God. But it proved difficult to sing at all. The words seemed to choke in my throat, and it was the same for everyone else.

No one could could have predicted that the pageant play would have the negative, demoralizing effect it did have, and afterwards (the whole thing lasted less than twenty minutes) we all felt more depressed than ever. After that it became harder and harder to make a joyful noise for any reason. Christmas, 1942, marked the end of the first phase of our incarceration at the Hotel Tacloban. The abject hopelessness of our predicament was driven home that day. The war had just begun, the Japanese still had the edge, and we sensed more clearly the ordeal that lay ahead. After Christmas, 1942, we began to feel the full force of Japanese oppression. Disease, malnutrition, exertion and stress began to take their toll.

Chapter Eleven

A dark cloud of melancoly hung over the Hotel Tacloban in the days following Christmas, 1942. The new year offered no hope of quick release, our spirits lay in pieces on the ground, and just being in camp became harder to bear. Tempers became frayed and a rash of fights errupted between the Aussies and the Brits, so, in an effort to purge ourselves of our mounting frustration, we resorted to making obscene gestures at the guards when their backs were turned or when we thought they weren't looking. We were forever devising new ways to defy the little bastards, even though those acts had little merit in themselves and accomplished nothing to improve our lot. But, due to the extreme monotony and cheerlessness, acts of defiance became our principle means of preserving our identity as soldiers, of relieving the tension, of lifting our spirits, and of stealing a laugh at the expense of the cruel Japanese.

In addition, I sincerely believed that, by taking risks, I was enhancing my status among the macho Australians. In my gut I felt that acts of defiance were the best way to gain and hold their respect. Unfortunately, the price I paid was very high. Case in point: one sundrenched afternoon in March of 1943, Clyde Merrit (one of our resident Diggers) and Peter Price (a mill hand from Sydney) invited Jassy and me to share a smoke behind Clyde's hut. (Incidentally, Clyde never lost weight. He kept his potbelly right up until the day he died of dysentery, several months later.) Clyde had somehow managed to appropriate one of the awful tasting, funnel-shaped cigarettes which now and then magically appeared in camp. I never knew where they came from or how they got into camp, and I never presumed to ask, but if one was being passed around I was always offered and always took a drag. The cigarettes themselves were made from stale, rancid leaves of locally grown, uncured tobacco; on the other hand, they contained nicotine, they had bite, and they did a lot to reduce hunger pains. So, despite their flaws, those of us who liked to smoke enjoyed them immensely, when we could get them. *That* was the catch.

Not only was it hard to find a cigarette, but the Major had also determined that smoking could be hazardous to our health, and he had officially banned it in certain areas at certain times. For instance, we weren't permitted to smoke when we were working, or when we were standing in line for rice, or when we were assembled for roll call (known as "stand-up" to the Aussies.) Due to dry leaves and the threat of fire, smoking was prohibited in our huts and we weren't allowed to litter, although every scrap of tobacco was automatically put to good use. Under *no* circumstances was it advisable to get caught with a cigarette in your hand by the guards or the Major, both of whom interpreted the act of smoking as a personal insult; as a result, we had to play hide-and-go-seek when we wanted to indulge, gathering in clandestine groups behind the huts, cupping the butt and passing it around furtively, like schoolboys in the lavatory. But if you liked smoking it was worth the risk.

On that particular day the four of us were huddled behind Clyde's hut, passing a butt and shooting the breeze. "Ain't it a fuckin' shame, 'ow them bloody Brits act like the sun rises and sets out o' the Major's bleedin' arse?" Clyde wondered out loud, inhaling deeply then passing the cigarette to Jassy, who received it enthusiastically. "It's a-nuff to piss the Pope."

"Too bloody right, mate," Jassy agreed, " 'is majesty the Major is *one* tight-arsed son-of-a-bitch." He quickly took a second puff, passed it to Pete.

"Wot a ruddy bastard 'e is, prowlin' 'round at night like a bloody bushwacker," Pete added, taking a long drag then handing the remainder to me.

There wasn't too much left by then, so I took a puff to keep it lit, looked around for something to say, and an idea popped into my head. Everyone I could see seemed to be doing something else. No one seemed to be paying any attention to us. The two guards at the main gate were dozing off in the heat, and the Major was nowhere to be seen, so, thinking the coast was clear, I said to the Aussies, "Watch this, fellas. I'm gonna run over to the fence and those little yellow bastards won't even see me." Smart, huh? Little did I know that, just then, the Major was rounding the corner of Clyde's hut. I took one last drag, raced over to the fence (treading over forbidden territory in the process), flipped the butt through the barbed wire, then ran back. It was a stupid thing to do. The guards didn't see me, but the Major did. He witnessed the whole damn episode, and the bastard reported me.

Nothing happened that day, and that was a bad sign. What I'd done was a serious infraction of the rules, as well as a direct slap in the Major's face, and I knew I was in deep trouble. There'd been an increasing number of incidents since Christmas, however, and in order to prove to Captain Yoshishito that he wasn't (despite appearances) losing control of the situation, the Major decided to teach us all a lesson, once and for all, by making an example out of me.

Everyone was assembled the following morning before breakfast. The Major, whose duty it was to preside over disciplinary matters, marched in front of us with the ranking British NCO, Sgt. Major Goodhall, at his side. Captain Yoshishito, accompanied by his junior officers, joined the Major, but I still didn't know what to expect. Then the Japanese guards pulled me out of ranks, stripped me naked, tied my hands behind my back, tied my ankles together, and tied a bandana across my mouth. Immediately my hands and feet began to swell and I started to suffocate. A Filipino interpretor was brought forward and I was informed that I would have to stand there at attention until sundown. Ten hours away. I was told that if I fainted or fell to the ground, I was finished. Dead.

The British junior officers had braced themselves for the inevitable and were cautiously avoiding my gaze. The Japanese appeared very serious, as usual. Behind me I heard grumblings from my comrades and my heart leaped into my throat. I looked at Duff for reassurance, but there was no offer of hope, only rage and anger in his face. I retreated within my-self, cleared my mind of fear, and waited for the fun to begin.

The human body dehydrates very quickly in the scorching heat of the tropical sun, and within an hour I began to feel the effects. I realized as the sun climbed higher into the sky, as the heat and light intensified, that I'd never make it. But the Japanese, on the Major's recommendation, wanted every-one else to be strong enough to witness my undoing, so pe-riodically they allowed small groups of prisoners to fall out of ranks for a drink of water. I tried to yell through the cloth they'd tied across my mouth that I needed water too, but it was a waste of energy. They weren't about to give *me* any. Instead, just to drive me crazy, they occasionally moistened the outside of the rag where it covered my mouth. I could feel the coolness seeping through the fabric, and I could taste moisture on my lips with the tip of my tongue, but it wasn't wet enough for me to suck water. My stomach got the message that water was on the way, but when none arrived, the effect was worse than no water at all. Waves of panic swept through me.

The Aussies, at that point, could see what was happening, that I wouldn't make it, and they started whooping and hol-lering to spur me on. It was a totally spontaneous thing. Some of the men were singing "Yankee Doodle," but they didn't know all the words so they repeated the first verse over and over, whistling and humming to the tune. I could feel them stirring behind me. I could sense their concern. Other men began to sing Christian hymns, and I heard one of the Brits in the background singing "The White Cliffs of Dover":*

> *I'll never forget the people I met,*
> *Braving those angry skies;*
> *I remember it well as the shadows fell,*
> *The light of hope in their eyes.*

*"The White Cliffs of Dover". Words by Nat Burton, music by Walter Kent. Copyright by Bernstein, Shapiro & Company, Inc., 1941; NYC, NY.

"Come on, Dougo," Jassy shouted. It sounded strange to hear my name mentioned. I closed my eyes.

"Hang in there, Yank," another man yelled. But my lungs were bursting and the blood was pounding in my head and suddenly everything began to spin. I lost my balance, fell forward, head first, and having no way to cushion the fall, landed flat on my face. I felt my nose break and I thought to myself, "Oh, my God! It's all over now," at the same time rolling over on my side and instinctively curling up in a ball in anticipation of the forthcoming blows. The Japanese guards were waiting for that. They instantly started kicking me and clubbing me with their rifle butts, screaming at me to get up or die. They kicked me over and over again in the stomach, crotch and kidneys, in my face and in my back. I heard one of my ribs crack, felt a searing pain shoot through my side. Meanwhile another guard kicked me viciously in the mouth, knocking out my front teeth, and I started choking on pieces of broken tooth that stuck in my throat. But I couldn't spit because of the cloth covering my mouth and I didn't know whether the warm blood I tasted was from the cracked teeth or from the broken rib. I did know that if I didn't get up soon, I was dead for sure.

To calm myself, I began reciting "The Lord's Prayer," and when I finished saying that I said "The 23rd Psalm." But even while I was praying I was thinking to myself "Oh, no! The Lord's not going to help me now. The only time I call upon Him is when I need help, like now." But there was nothing else I could do. My hands and feet were bound and the Japanese were pounding me into the ground.

Behind me the Aussies were going crazy with rage, shouting out words of encouragement, cursing the Japanese and the Major and the Brits, singing hymns and army songs, creating a commotion far more violent than anything the Japanese had expected or were prepared to deal with. Suddenly the blows stopped falling on my body; from the corner of my eye I could see agitated guards running up and down the line of prisoners, screaming and yelling at them, shoving them with their rifle butts, poking them with their bayonets, motioning wildly at them to get back inside their huts. But every time the Japanese guards corralled one group of Aussies in a hut, another group would spill out into the prison yard, whooping and hooting and shouting "Coooeee!" like Comanches on the warpath.

The guards had turned their attention away from me when the Aussies started rioting, allowing me the opportunity to roll over on my back, to relieve a measure of the excruciating pain in my side. As I lay there breathless, panting, my eyes shut tight, I could hear Jeff Connelly singing "Amazing Grace." In a moment everyone had joined in, either singing or humming or whistling, their scrambled voices combining to sound, through the ringing in my ears, like the ghostly skirl of bagpipes:

> Amazing Grace, how sweet the sound,
> That saved a wretch like me.
> I once was lost, but now am found,
> Was blind but now can see.*

What happened next sounds crazy, I know. I was lying on my back, listening to the Aussies and squinting into the glaring sun, when a remote voice emanated from the blinding light that flashed across the sky, commanding me to rise. Hands felt gently beneath me, lifting me off the ground, and even though my hands and feet were bound—even though I'd been beaten senseless—I found myself standing. And I stayed up. And I stayed up until even those Japanese bastards felt ashamed and stood in awe. Sensing that his plan had backfired, Captain Yoshishito signalled to his subordinates, who then ordered my comrades to carry me back to my quarters. Jassy and Travis quickly stepped forward and led me back to our hut. Much to the Major's dismay, I'd survived. I'll never understand how, or why, but I did.

And then the Aussies sent up a cheer. They whooped and they hollered and they swore on everything sacred to Australians that that no-good English son-of-a-bitch was going to pay. There'd been plenty of instances prior to this when

*"Amazing Grace": words and music by John Newton (18th century).

88

the Japanese had abused prisoners; men were missing teeth and ears and eyes; men were limping around lame and twisted from unset, broken bones; men were immobilized with infected wounds from being used as ashtrays, punching bags, even for bayonet practice; but up until now it had all been initiated by the Japanese. This was the first time the Major had gone so far as to personally intervene to punish someone so severely for such a minor crime. He didn't have to inform on me, or have me used as a scapegoat, but he did. Consequently, the Aussies blamed the Major, not the Japanese. His actions that day caused a reversal in our thinking; from that fateful day on, the hatred toward the Major turned to poison.

Chapter Twelve

Unlike the well-trained combat troops I'd tangled with in the jungles of New Guinea, the guards at the Hotel Tacloban were the dregs of the Japanese Army. It was obvious that they resented having been exiled to our backwater POW camp—that they blamed *us* directly for their misfortune—and the general consensus of opinion was that we'd have fared much better if our guards had been regular soldiers. As it was, we were subjected to the perverted whims of frustrated, amateur soldiers with no empathy for our plight. Midget conquistadors myopically imagining their peaked caps to be crowns, our deluded guards were totally unaware of how ridiculous they looked strutting around camp like bantams in a pine wood. To the bitter end they remained convinced of their innate racial superiority.

Approximately two dozen guards were quartered in the barracks at any given time, with each detachment of guards staying for an average eight-month tour of duty, or until such time as fresh troops arrived on the scene to take their places. The replacements kept getting older and meaner and, as the war steadily turned against Japan, they kept getting more and more intent upon unleashing their personal and national frustrations on us. Depending on the prevailing mood of the camp, or on the attitude of a particular batch of guards, we were required to stand at attention and lower our heads whenever a guard passed by. This was done in part to humiliate us, and in part because our guards, none of whom were combat veterans, were more afraid of the Aussies than we were of them. Based on propaganda (not completely unfounded) they'd been fed by their commanding officers, our guards thought the Aussies were homocidal maniacs who were just itching for a chance to slit their throats, and so they always circulated in pairs, and they took care to avoid the shadows.

As to be expected, the Aussies had nicknames for all the

guards. The Japanese NCO in charge of the guards, and the one Japanese enlisted man never rotated out of camp, was dubbed Yellow Flake in honor of the tiny yellow specks which flickered in the whites of his eyes whenever he was riled, which was often. We suspected Tokyo Rose, a real sweetheart of a sadist, of being a closet homosexual, and then there was Shit Pants, an unbelievably skinny man whose pants always seemed to be sagging from a fresh load of crap. Over time, as we got to know each of them individually, one of our favorite sources of entertainment was using the language barrier as a foil to make fun of our humorless guards. For instance, any prisoner could say (if he wore a contrite expression on his face), "Yes, sir, honorable Shit Pants," then stifle a laugh and go about his business. And they never got the joke.

The Japanese Camp Commandant, Captain Yoshishito, did not conform to any of the usual stereotypes; he didn't wear thick glasses and he didn't squint; he didn't have buck teeth, bandy legs, or a moon face; and he didn't throw infantile temper tantrums when he received bad news. On the contrary, Captain Yoshishito was tall and thin, rather handsome, intelligent, scholarly and sullenly aloof. His uniform was nicely tailored, his manners faultlessly refined, and, although he was ill-at-ease in his role as Camp Commandant and was obviously not a professional soldier, he played upon our high-strung Major the way a virtuoso plays upon a fine violin. For above all, Captain Yoshishito was a purebred Japanese aristocrat who considered *all* Caucasians lower than dirt.

According to Duff, Masumi Yoshishito had been a school administrator in civilian life, a profession at which he excelled and a profession which, by enabling him to help shape Japan's youth in conformity with its emerging self-image as the dominant military, economic, and cultural force in the Far East, afforded him a deep sense of personal satisfaction. Little did Yoshishito know, however, that he too had been subliminally indoctrinated by the deluge of nationalistic propaganda that began flooding Japan in the early 1930s, with the invasion of Manchuria. Like most of his credulous countrymen, Yoshishito never dreamed that Emperor Hirohito (the divine monarch worshipped as God incarnate by his fanatic Shinto

followers) was more of a puppet than a deity. He never realized that the military pulled the Emperor's strings; he knew
only that the Emperor wanted him to join the Holy Crusade
to drive the demonic, imperialistic White race (Germans excluded) from all of Asia. And if his beloved Emperor wished
him to fight, then he would fight, gladly. If his Emperor
called upon him to lay down his life for the glory of Japan,
then Yoshishito was perfectly willing to die. It was that simple.

Waging war was justifiable, as always, on the basis of moral
ascendency; the sacred Japanese mission to unite Asia was
merely the Yellow man's version of the White man's burden.
To pave the way for its incursions into China in 1937, the
military machine in Japan used the national press to stir up
anti-Chinese sentiment. Likewise, by using advertising tech-
niques developed on Madison Avenue, the Japanese Army
filled its ranks with gullible young men like Masumi Yoshishito, who, when Pearl Harbor was bombed and war was
declared in December of 1941, unhesitatingly resigned his post
as school administrator, joined the Imperial Japanese Army
and embraced Bushido, "the way of the warrior," a Spartan
lifestyle stressing self-denial, bravery, blind obedience to superiors, and suicide before dishonor.

In view of his professional background, but at the expense
of his individuality (if such a concept exists in Japanese philosophy), Yoshishito quickly advanced to the rank of captain.
And once enrolled in the universal brotherhood of officers,
he realized that tax dollars were being wasted on public education and other social services; what was really required
were huge increases in "defense" spending. Suddenly he didn't
mind that civil rights were sacrificed in the name of national
security. The man who believed in academic freedom accepted
censorship for the common good. So what if the nation danced
to military music!? Yoshishito truly believed that the Emperor
was calling the tune. He continued to hold fast to his con-
victions even when (based on his management abilities) he
was awarded the dubious honor of being made prison warden
in backwater Leyte. It didn't matter (much) to him; he du-
tifully obeyed all orders as if they had originated with Emperor Hirohito himself. Captain Yoshishito even went so far

as to carry out orders, issued by his superiors in Tokyo, commanding him to commit all manner of gruesome atrocities on prisoners. I'd like to think that he did so reluctantly.

I sincerely believe that Captain Yoshishito and his staff were no more responsible for what happened on that tiny plot of earth, to which we were all confined, than I am for the things we did in response. Nevertheless, I can't pretend that the bitterness doesn't persist. It's a sad testimony to intrinsic human nature, the savage way they mistreated us, and it was years before I could understand how anyone could have any regard for the Japanese. Maybe people just don't know what they did to POWs, or maybe they just don't give a damn. Maybe there's no reason why they should. It's been explained to me that the typical Japanese soldier felt no remorse for the atrocities he committed—that the group expected him to do it and that if he didn't do it, he felt only failure, inadequacy, and shame. I'm told that the Japanese are inherently different from us and cannot be judged by Western standards. On the other hand, I've experienced first-hand the Japanese philosophy about dealing out pain to inferior races, and I've watched them giggle while my comrades writhed in agony, then died. I can forgive them, maybe. But I can never forget. To this day, whenever I chance to meet a Japanese, I'm seized by an overpowering urge to attack and I must exercise all of my self-restraint until the feeling passes. You just can't imagine what they put us through.

There's a widespread perception that the Japanese nation was the innocent victim of atomic warfare—that noncombatants suffered a fate reserved for soldiers, and that the punishment exceeded the crime. And maybe that's true. But it's also true that many more POWs and soldiers, maybe as many as one million, would have died if the bombs had not been dropped. In case you didn't know, in the summer of 1945 the Supreme Japanese Commander, Field Marshall Terauchi, ordered all POWs killed, if and when the Allies invaded the Japanese mainland. Ironically, Hiroshima and Nagasaki averted that tragedy. Indeed, at the risk of being called anti-Asiatic or racist by enlightened people, I must confess that for many years I secretly wished that more bombs had been dropped on Japan. There was a time in my life when I wished their nation had been completely destroyed.

At this point I'd like to try to put my own experience into some sort of historical perspective, not as justification for my feelings, but to set the stage for what eventually did happen at the Hotel Tacloban. Let me begin by saying that by the spring of 1942, more than 130,000 English, Australian and American soldiers had fallen into Japanese hands, most of whom were lost at Singapore when the English Officer commanding, General Arthur E. Percival, refused to construct defenses along Singapore's northern beaches because, in his opinion, doing so would have been bad for the morale of soldiers and civilians. Of the nearly 20,000 Aussies captured during World War Two, more than one-third perished in captivity. The percentage, notably, was smaller among the Brits.

An estimated 12,000 American soldiers were captured on Bataan Peninsula (which is across the Bay from Manila at the extreme southern tip of Luzon, the principal island of the Philippines). Their commander, General Douglas MacArthur, said about these men in his famous autobiography, *Reminscences*: "Their hoarse, wild laughter greeted the constant stream of obscene and ribald jokes issuing from parched, dry throats. They cursed the enemy and in the same breath they cursed and reviled the United States; they spat when they jeered at the Navy...They were filthy and they were lousy and they stank. And I loved them."* "Dougout Doug" loved them and left them. Left them to pay the price of resistance while, with his family and a few top aides, he snuck off to Australia, leaving behind only a promise to keep the soldier's faith and to return, someday.

"We're the Battling Bastards of Bataan: no momma, no poppa, no Uncle Sam," that's what the men MacArthur abandoned said about themselves. Twenty percent of them died on the Death March from Mariveles to Camp O'Donnell,

*(McGraw-Hill, New York, 1964; pages 135-136.)

most bayoneted or beaten to death by the vindictive Japanese soldiers they'd fought tooth and nail for the past four months. There was no general issue of food or water for a week and many men starved along the way; all were forced to drink from streams polluted by bloated corpses. Mutilated, charred bodies of crucified comrades hung upside down from trees lining the route. Filipino on-lookers who dared to toss scraps of food to the prisoners were shot offhand. Prisoners were banded in groups of ten and if one escaped the rest were killed. Several men did in fact escape, but those who tried and failed were forced to kneel and bend over, then were bayoneted in their rectums.

Survivors of the Death March were transported like cattle in boxcars to Cabanatuan, where men too weak from dysentery, exhaustion and malnutrition to go out on work details died of thirst, unless they could afford to buy sections of bamboo filled with water and plugged at both ends from fellow prisoners who were strong enough to venture out and work. The going price for a drink was ten dollars. One unfortunate soldier was kept in a bamboo cage at the main gate as a warning to all who entered. The cage was too low for the man to stand upright, so he crawled in his own feces on his hands and knees, spitting and barking at anyone who approached. Bemused Japanese guards fed him scraps of garbage for three months, until he curled up in a corner and died. The Japanese guards left his decomposing body inside the cage for another two weeks as a reminder to his outraged comrades.

During the first month at Cabanatuan, fifty to sixty men died daily from dysentery alone, with those under the age of twenty-five succumbing first. The death rate among enlisted men, incidentally, was five times as high on the average as it was among officers, who lived apart, ate better, and were not abused. It's no wonder that prisoners gladly volunteered for work crews heading off for faraway places like Pusan in Korea, Mukden in Manchuria, and Tientsin in China. Anything to escape Cabanatuan. Some men ended up in Malaya, Burma, or Thailand working on the infamous railroad along with Aussies and Brits captured at Singapore. Others were shuffled off to Bilibid on Luzon, or Bukidnon or Davao Penal Colony on Mindanao. Still others were sent to camps such as Honshu in Japan to serve as examples of Western decadence, while others rotted away in obscurity in Bandoeng in Java. Everywhere it was the same: sickness, torture and death.

Compared to the approximately 250,000 Allied POWs interned in German and Italian camps, of whom only four percent died in captivity, with the 130,000 or so POWs taken by the Japanese, thirty percent never returned. For those of us in POW camps in the Far East, there was but a negligible chance of escape or release before the end of the war, and that made it easier to give up hope altogether. We sat in our hovels, slowly wasting away, wondering what the hell was going on "out there," or if anyone even cared. As a matter of fact, thanks in part to military censorship, not too many people in 1942 and 1943 were losing sleep over POWs and MIAs; even the military itself was more concerned with turning the tables on the Japanese (which, in all fairness, was no easy trick) than it was rescuing men it had already written off. There was that all-important "winning" public image to maintain, and that took preference over the facts. (Unpopular wars are hard to finance—remember Vietnam?) So, rather than casting a defeatist pall over the Big Picture, the military accentuated the positive and eliminated the negative when it came to reporting the ungodly nature of the war in the Pacific, thereby keeping the American public (as it prefers) blissfully in the dark concerning POWs rotting away in captivity. As long as people continued to believe the sanitized accounts they read in the newspapers (control of information is the crux of any authority—it's an end in itself), they would continue to support those who were running the war.

Please bear with me for a moment while I present a brief summary of what was happening in late 1942 and 1943.

On November 6, 1942, General Douglas MacArthur moved his HQ to Moresby, thereby taking the first step in his pledged return to the Philippines. Bravo! Six days later his arch-rival in New Guinea, General Horii, drowned while crossing the Kumusi River at a point less than twenty miles from Buna; having failed to take his objective, Horii's death may well have been a suicide. On November 17, Horii's replacement, Colonel Yamamoto, arrived in Gona from Rabaul with about one thousand reinforcements but, faced with defeat, he committed hari-kari on January 2, 1943, on the same day the American 126th Regiment took Bloody Buna from fanatical Japanese soldiers who fought to the last man. The myth of the invincible Nipponese soldier was permanently laid to rest at Buna, thanks to the 32nd Division, which had the honor of claiming the US Army's first ground campaign victory of the war. Casualties, however, numbered 90 percent of total strength of the division when it went into combat, and of the men in my unit only a handful survived. After Buna, the 32nd was sent down under to Australia for a well-deserved rest.

Meanwhile, American and Australian forces under MacArthur continued to grind ahead. Cape Endaiadere, Giropa Point and Soputa fell in 1942. On January 20, 1943, the Japanese relinquished Sanananda to the Allies; Colonel Yazawa, whose troops had captured me three months earlier, was himself killed during the Japanese retreat to Lae. Woodlark Island and the Trobriands, both in the Solomon Sea, fell to MacArthur's forces in June. Other victories in 1943 included: Lae and Salamaua in New Guinea; Arawe on New Britain; Long Island in the Bismarck Sea; and Finschhafen, which fell to the Aussies in October.

Elsewhere, while MacArthur's forces were leap-frogging along New Guinea's northern coast, the US Marines were mopping up on Guadalcanal. On February 21, the Leathernecks stormed ashore on the Russel Islands, and by the end of 1943 they'd chalked up victories on Rendova, New Georgia, Vella Lavella, Choiseul and the Treasury Group, Makin in the Gilberts, Tarawa Atoll, Cape Glouster and Bouganville. By the beginning of 1944, the Allies already were converging on MacArthur's ultimate goal, the Philippines.

In response to Allied offensives in New Guinea and the Solomons, the majority of Japanese troops on Leyte were withdrawn and shipped to battlefields in the South Pacific, so that by the spring of 1943 a mere token force of about five hundred soldiers remained on the island. Responsible for managing a population of close to one million, this small contingent of Japanese troops was compelled to limit its activities to patrol of the coast and control of Tacloban and the San Juanico Strait. The hinterlands were temporarily abandoned to Filipino insurgents and, in the vacuum left behind by the hard-pressed Japanese, guerrilla bands began to emerge. Wary of showing themselves, these guerrilla bands periodically emerged from hiding, when it was safe, to disrupt the flow of food to Tacloban or to assasinate some overly enthusiastic collaborationist; but for the most part, as I've already explained, they were fully engaged in a protracted struggle for supremacy among themselves.

Before the Allies could make serious plans for a Philippine re-invasion, they first had to galvanize these foundering guerrilla factions into a coherent whole. The most difficult obstacle to overcome, in doing this, was establishing an effective chain of command—in other words, figuring out which chieftan on any given island was the most trustworthy. On Leyte the man voted most likely to succeed was Colonel Rupert Kangleon, a powerful warlord based in the southern part of the island. As was the case with guerrilla leaders throughout the Philippines, Colonel Kangleon was furnished by the Allies with arms, ammunition, medical supplies and radios, and was promised a position of power in the postwar Philippine government, in exchange for keeping track of Japanese shipping and collecting valuable information on Japanese troop strength and placements, all of which was radioed back to Allied Intelligence HQ in Australia. As part of the deal, Colonel Kangleon was also expected to make contact with POWs near Tacloban. Whether he did or did not is a question of tremendous importance to me. Unfortunately, it is a question which remains unanswered.

I do know that a guerrilla network similar to Kangleon's was established on Mindanao, and that in the spring of 1943 it provided several American POWs with the means to escape Davao Penal Colony. These fortunate men made it safely to Australia with the first eyewitness reports of prison life in the Philippines. However, when the braided caps in Washington read these reports, they immediately slammed the lid on them.

The Allies were committed to winning the war in Europe first; assuming that American public opinion, if it knew the truth, would call for a greater effort against the Japanese (which was something they wanted to postpone until after Hitler was on the run), the bigwigs in Washington, under pressure from the English, stifled all reports detailing the extent of atrocities committed in Japanese POW camps.

Meanwhile, the only other way to help POWs was through covert action; therefore, special Intelligence agents were deposited on every major island in the Philippines. Traveling in submarines from bases in Australia, rendezvousing with guerrillas at pre-arranged times and places, paddling ashore in rubber rafts under cover of darkness, these highly trained commandos supplied the guerrillas with the tools of their trade. They also, for propaganda purposes, distributed candy bars, cigarettes and matches, and leaflets signed by MacArthur which read, "I shall return," to the civilian population. On Mindanao, Allied agents aided by existing guerrillas contacted POWs at Davao Penal Colony prompting a second, aborted escape attempt in which several men were re-captured and summarily executed. That was in March, 1944. I have reason to believe that Allied agents may have tried to pull off a similar stunt on Leyte at the close of the previous year.

Two other events of significance were unfolding at the end of 1943. First, Japanese reinforcements were pouring back into the Philippines in anticipation of the inevitable re-invasion; on Leyte, approximately 5,000 Japanese soldiers had arrived by December, had driven the still squabbling guerrillas back into the hills, and were once again in firm control of the island. With that, the hammer came down hard. A martial state was created in which the Imperial Japanese Army had priority over everything, and everyone else starved. To win Filipino hearts and minds, the Japanese did allow the collaborationist regime in Manila (headed by José Laurel) to declare long-awaited Philippine independence, but in the wake of the US Naval blockade (the second significant event), hollow political gestures meant nothing to the Filipinos. American submarines were sinking any and all merchant ships which attempted to bring food and supplies into Leyte—conditions were so bad that alcohol extracted from tuba (distilled palm juice) was being used as a substitute for gasoline.

In any event, transportation was the least of our problems at the Hotel Tacloban.

Chapter Thirteen

1943 was a particularly bad year at the Hotel Tacloban. Unlike the vast majority of Japanese POW camps, whose inmates benefited from a steady influx of new prisoners bearing news of recent Allied successes, we were completely cutoff from the outside world. I was the last man to enter camp. And whereas some of the larger camps received letters and packages from home, or in some cases maintained hidden radios, in all the time I was imprisoned at the Hotel Tacloban, not one of us even received a letter or a Red Cross package or any other piece of information at all. Nothing. And yet, although this total isolation was in many ways our worst psychological oppressor, it did serve one positive function: there was never any cause for the cynical exploitation of the weak by the strong which debased so many other POW camps. We had no possessions to fight over, no commerce to compete for, all articles of value (including watches, wallets, and jewelry) having been confiscated immediately by the Japanese guards, who then bartered their booty for rice wine in Tacloban. We had no coins or paper money (we used little chits when we played cards or gambled) and it would have been impossible to buy things like eggs or vegetables or tobacco, even if we did have money. Floods in the spring of 1943 had wiped out the local food supply and, what with the naval blockade, there was none to spare. Furthermore, the only Filipinos in camp were collaborationists assisting the Japanese in its day-to-day operation, and even if one of us had been able to speak their language, doing so was strictly forbidden, under penalty of death.

Nevertheless, because there was limited commerce between the guards and the Filipinos in camp, it is possible that some things did pass through the guards to the POWS, although I can't imagine what bribes the prisoners could have offered in exchange. I doubt that the Japanese were being generous. That wasn't their style. And I doubt that Filipino collaborationists met secretly with POWs inside the barbed wire, although that too remains a possibility.

We'd run out of kerosene and candle wax by the spring of 1943 during the second, the "hatred," phase of our imprisonment. We were running low on conversation, too. It was impossible to play cribbage anymore, because the cards were dog-eared and soggy and you knew every card your opponent held in his hand. There was no privacy and nothing to do except fight among ourselves, take dangerous chances, and dream of escape.

The Major and his henchmen were patrolling the camp at irregular hours, looking for trouble, and we never knew when they were going to show up for a head-count so we didn't want to leave our huts at night, not even to take a piss. We didn't know where anyone was at anymore. Suspicion gripped the entire camp. By necessity we developed the knack for recognizing noises, for knowing that it was the guards passing by on their hourly rounds, not some Aussie sneaking from one hut to another. We'd awake at a sudden drop in barometric pressure or at a slight rise in the wind. The tension was almost unbearable.

Under this aura of repression the peculiar habits of others, magnified as they were by close confinement, became personally insulting. Like everyone else in camp I lay awake at night, restless and keyed-up, and my mind would start to wander. Each night I retreated into an elaborate fantasy world of my own design—an elegant brothel in the gaudy French Quarter of New Orleans where I let my imagination run amok. Rubenesque nudes graced oak paneled walls; I walked on plush magenta carpets; reclined on satin sheets and fluffy pillows; ate scrumptious meals on clean blue china plates; and when I tried hard enough, I could even feel the soft flesh of voluptuous harlots indulging my every erotic desire. Afterwards I luxuriated under a hard, hot shower for a long, long time. (By the way, the Aussies never lost any sleep imagining showers; never having had an opportunity to use one, they didn't know what they were missing.)

Although I felt the longings as much as any normal teen-ager, sex, or the lack thereof, was never a major problem for me. For starters, we were surrounded by sensations which conspired to offend, not to excite; lack of nutritional food, disease and exhaustion, the sight of broken, tormented men, the constant harassment and tension and the repulsive living conditions forced upon us, all combined to nullify a man's libido. The visual stimulation wasn't there, either; the Japanese guards never imported prostitutes into camp, and we rarely saw Filipino women passing by on Highway 1. My biggest fear was, as the old saying goes, "If you don't use it, you lose it," although in time even that concern faded away. In time the topic of sex vanished altogether.

As to homosexuality, there wasn't as much as one might expect, it being beyond the conceptual range of the average Australian soldier at the time to imagine that one of his mates might be queer and we developed a code of behavior in that regard which was acceptable to everyone—the men who were so inclined segregated themselves from the rest of us and were left in peace. Of course I was only seventeen at the time, and very naive, and there may have been things going on that I wasn't aware of; but I wasn't interested, and it was none of my business, and none of the men in my hut were involved, so it was never a significant issue as far as I was concerned.

I chose to take the high road in satisfying my need for meaningful contact with my comrades, and once Duff had expressed an interest in getting to know me, I regularly sought him out for stimulating conversation. It would have been a gross breach of Australian etiquette to approach him directly in public, however (*that* would have been misconstrued as currying favor—an intolerable sin among the Aussies), so I'd casually stick my head in his hut if I happened to be passing by, and I'd say, "Hey, Duff! Got time to talk?" And if he was alone and not too busy (and not having headaches) he'd invite me inside for a chat. He'd stand up from the little table he had, close the medical text he was always reading, then we'd sit together on his pad (as was the custom in camp when two men were having a private conversation) and we'd talk until the inevitable emergency called him away. But before he left he'd say, "Let's finish this chat later on, okay?" Duff never closed the door on me, and I always left his presence feeling better.

Duff was an intellectually curious man who was fascinated by everything American, especially our schools, and he jumped at the chance to pick my brain. He wanted to learn what our regional differences were, what I'd been taught in school, and what I knew about Australia—which amounted to a whole lot less than what Duff knew about America. For instance: I'd been taught, correctly, that Australia had a Socialist government. But I'd also been told that all Socialists were mindless marionettes, and the reality of Australian independence astounded me, as did the Aussie version of egalitarian society; as Duff explained it, a pro-labor government aiming for full employment—the Robin Hood School of Economics, wherein the rich are taxed mightily to provide services for the poor.

The more we talked, the more we found we had in common, including a love of literature. It was a part of his personality he kept close to his vest, perhaps revealing only to me, but Duff had a special fondness for Charles Dickens and Edgar Allan Poe. There were other instances too when Duff had trouble relating to his salt-of-the-earth countrymen, and because he could discuss subjects with me which were of little interest to the other men, he seemed to value our chats almost as much as I did. Duff was the first well-educated person I'd ever been able to form a relationship with, and the little time I spent with him (once or twice a month) was in many ways spiritually sustaining.

Duff was my pressure-release valve; talking with him took up the slack in my lonely life and it gave me a chance to get the things that were bothering me off my chest. It gave me a chance to talk about death—a subject which was hard to avoid at the Hotel Tacloban, a subject which preoccupied my thoughts. Thoughts which seemed beyond my control. One minute I was up, the next I was down, and yet I always returned to square one—uncertainty. But Duff was a man who dealt primarily with facts, and by transmitting a portion of his knowledge to me, he helped me to put my thoughts about death into perspective, to achieve a welcome measure of balance.

"Everyone thinks he's an island," Duff once remarked. "Each one of us thinks that death is for everyone else but himself. Just look around you. What do you see? Death is everywhere, and yet you know you're going to survive."

He was right. I did feel that way.

"I'm sure I'm going to make it through this thing," he stated matter-of-factly, then added, "and I'm sure you'll make it too."

It was very reassuring to know that someone I admired had faith in me. It bolstered my spirits. "But you know," I said back to him, "sometimes death seems like to only decent way out of this madness. I wonder, why not just accept it?"

"Because death always comes too soon," he replied cheerfully, "and that's the joke. Each one of us...why, we're just kidding ourselves. Our lives here mean nothing, if "living" means having some purpose as we pass from day to day. It's conceit that confuses us.

"Listen," he continued, "staying alive is the only way you have of defying those little yellow bastards out there. It's the only purpose you have. They want you to give up without a fight. The Major, too. They make death available. Christ Almighty! They shove it down our throats! Fuck 'em, Doug. Stay alive. You've got to hang on to your life."

In my chats with Duff, I learned a lot about the Major and the English, about Captain Yoshishito and the Japanese, and about the Aussies, too. The insights he handed me made them all easier to bear, easier to understand, and the flow of ideas and information between us was a welcome release from the numbing boredom of prison life, too. But of course not all of our conversations were philosophical, or agreeable, and part of the fun was arguing. Especially where the subject of music was concerned.

Music was another sore spot for the Aussies. There's no denying that by the time a song reached the bush it was, to say the least, dated. The Brits considered the Aussies to be way behind the times, absolutely "prehistoric" is the term they used, when it came to popular music. On top of that, one of the Brits was the best singer in camp, a universally-recognized fact which allowed the Brits to lead our hymns during Sunday Worship service. In the rivalry between the two this was just one more feather in the British cap—a fact of life they never let the Aussies forget.

This is not to imply that the Hotel Tacloban was filled with voices raised in song. Not at all. Most of the time we were much too depressed to sing. But when a song was forthcoming, the Aussies usually rendered old favorites like, "Roll Out The Barrel," or, "The Wild Colonial Boy," or, "Bless Them All." Other standbys included Aussie army songs of a decidedly bawdy nature, and barroom ballads sung in husky baritone. To my surprise, melodic songs like "Do I Love You," and, "In The Still Of The Night," by Cole Porter were big hits popular with the Aussies as well, as were songs by Jerome Kern, such as "Lovely To Look At," and, "All The Things You Are."

Like anyone else, the Aussies had their musical prejudices too. For example, "Waltzing Matilda," which is often re-garded in America as the Australian national anthem, lacked the light-heartedness needed to be sung for fun, and it was *not* a popular song. Duff, whose accent was not nearly as thick as his mates, turned up his nose and called it "an Aus-tralian peasant song." But I liked it and thought it had prom-ise, and I foolishly suggested that it might even, with proper orchestration, sound good. The Aussies thought I was com-promising them—most had never heard it played on anything other than a banjo or harmonica or honky-tonk piano in some smoky Queensland saloon—and they scoffed at my sugges-tion that "Waltzing Matilda" had potential popular appeal. Duff and the other Aussies called me an asshole kid, said, "Wot does 'e know?" and laughed it off.

How did that make me feel? Like an outsider—like a fool. Despite my feeling strongly that we had a special understand-ing and a special friendship, Duff was ultimately more at ease with his countrymen, and it was the same with Travis and Jassy, too. Maybe it was out of loyalty to their roots, I'm not sure, but they were reluctant to take me into their con-fidence regarding camp intrigues; and that hurt. At times I felt excluded from the club—I felt a wrenching sense of rejection from the men I loved, and that exacerbated my profound loneliness. There was no one with a background like mine, no Bobby or Charley I could talk to without feeling self-conscious. The Aussies didn't know, or care, that Sid Luckman was quarterback for the Chicago Bears—they thought footballs were round—all of which made me feel lonelier than anyone else in that godforsaken deathtrap.

Unlike the relatively unenterprising men in my hut, Duff always had smokes (at least until the blockade squeezed us dry), and he'd always light up in my presence. One day in the summer of 1943, following one of our little chats, he actually gave me a few for my private consumption. Under the circumstances, it was the highlight of my career as a POW at the Hotel Tacloban. Smoking was the greatest pleasure I knew in that hellhole, and enjoying one in private was an experience that bordered on rapture. That very same afternoon I snuck behind my hut to have one, knowing full well that I was tempting fate, but heedless of the danger. To my everlasting regret, I was caught by the guards.

For some reason they were incensed and they went on a rampage, slapping me, whacking me with their rifle butts and poking me with their bayonets all the way to the Doghouse. But they were merely privates acting on their own initiative, and I didn't consider what I'd done to be *that* serious of an offense, so I didn't think they'd report me. I figured they'd leave me in the Doghouse for the rest of the day, as usual, or maybe overnight at most, then release me in the morning. Unfortunately, they did report me to their superiors and word of my misconduct reached the Major. Stricter punitive measures were deemed in order.

Now the Doghouse had been strategically placed in the center of the prison yard so that the cries and whimpers issuing forth could be heard by everyone in camp. The roof was made from a sheet of corrugated tin and the walls were of a durable wood like teak or mahogany, making it a virtual oven inside. There was no light, no ventilation, and no bucket for relieving yourself. The stench was toxic. To top it off, it was only four feet cubed; neither high enough to stand up, nor long enough to lie down. The only thing I could do was to sit there hunched over, my knees tucked under my chin, squirming, swatting flies, picking bugs off my scalp, nursing my bruises and cursing myself for being so stupid.

Nevertheless, I thought I'd be okay. I'd been in it two or three times before without experiencing any major problems, and almost every Australian had been thrown inside at one time or another, and no one had died yet. (Incidentally, such was the nature of justice at the Hotel Tacloban that on only one occasion was a Brit sent to the Doghouse, whereas, by the time we were rescued, I'd been in it six or seven times myself.) The Japanese guards usually kept us in it for between twelve and twenty-four hours, and I was sure that I could get through that intact.

This time, however, they kept me inside for two full days, during which time I received no food or water. (My only clue for determining just how long I was inside was that it grew somewhat darker and cooler at night.) But I still believed that being stuffed inside the Doghouse was going to be the extent of my punishment, and that hope enabled me to get through. But I was wrong. The worst was yet to come.

When the guards finally opened the door and ordered me out, I was so stiff from being cramped in a sitting position for forty-eight hours that it was impossible for me to bend my back to stand up straight and walk. I felt like I was wrapped in iron chains, and what with the blinding glare of the sunlight, I didn't move fast enough to suit the guards. The spiteful bastards immediately began hitting me with their rifle butts, prompting me to move along. They pushed me and shoved me across the prison yard to the cinder-block building that served as their barracks, then led me into a room in the rear. I'd never been in that building before, and I was having trouble focusing my vision and I felt nauseous from lack of food and water, so I was very uptight. The room itself was bare of funiture, except for an ominous bamboo platform about a foot and a half high in the center. On the platform were a sturdy wooden chair, a wooden bucket, and a swagger stick, the type carried by Japanese officers. The swagger stick was made out of tightly-wound strands of leather, like an English riding crop only stiffer, and it had a two-inch long loop at one end. It was an instrument of pain.

Not one word was spoken. Instead, just to heighten my concern and to lower my resistance, the guards made me stand there at attention for over an hour, until a tiny Filipino man entered the room, stepped carefully over the bamboo platform, picked up the swagger stick in both hands and began to fondle it. It was hard to judge just how old he was—people in the tropics age rapidly—but he looked to be about forty. He was thin and wrapped in ugly, brown, wax-paper skin, and he was shorter than the average Japanese, under five feet tall, but he was an exceedingly mean man, a psychopathic killer who wasn't bothered at all by rendering unto others a great deal of pain, a sadistic son-of-a-bitch the Aussies had nicknamed the Enforcer.

The Enforcer moved in front of me and stood there with his legs splayed, caressing the smooth leather of the swagger stick with his hands. Looking directly into my eyes, he whacked it menacingly against the side of his leg, smiled provocatively, then motioned to the guards, who stripped me naked, pushed me over the platform and gestured at me to sit down on the chair, the center of which had been cut out, like a toilet seat. Dizzy from hunger, weary from standing and teetering on the verge of collapse, I meekly did what they wanted, my genitals dropping down below my buttocks, exposed. Quickly the guards tied my wrists together behind the back of the chair, tied my ankles to the bottom rung, shoved the wooden bucket between my legs and returned to their posts on either side of the door, grinning eagerly. By then I knew exactly what to expect; the only unanswered question was whether or not they were planning to kill me, too.

The Enforcer was standing in front of me giggling shrilly the way Filipinos do when they're excited, only his giggle was louder than any I'd ever heard before. It was a sub-human squeal of delight that made me cringe. Without taking his eyes away from mine, he moved slowly around the platform until he was out of sight, and then, still giggling in anticipation, he gently, almost lovingly began to tap my penis and testicles with the loop end of the swagger stick. My entire body shuddered, tensed, errupted in a cold sweat. I clenched my teeth, recalling how the Japanese had mutilated my comrades on patrol, preparing myself for a similar fate. Likewise, what was happening to me now had no justification. It was something far more perverse than torture for the sake of eliciting military secrets. It was the result of a sickness so foul, so repulsive, that no amount of human rationalizing could ever wipe away its stain. The little bastard was sexually aroused and he started panting, and, as his breathing grew heavier, as his pleasure increased, so too did the force of his blows. And yet he seemed to know just how hard to hit me so I wouldn't faint.

At first the throbbing, indescribable pain was limited to my genitals, but as he continued to lash out, it spread to my abdomen, sending my empty stomach into violent convulsions. I heaved my guts up into the pail, then began to throw my weight from side to side, thinking that if I could somehow manage to rock the chair off the platform, that I might land on my head and knock myself out. But the legs seemed set in concrete, and I was too weak, too paralyzed by pain, to tip the chair over. And still the Enforcer's blows intensified. Bolts of lightning shot into arms and legs, my chest and my heart and my throat, until I began to choke on the pain, until I could no longer scream above the hurt that was tearing my body apart, until I could no longer feel the individual blows. But I could hear the bastard laughing. His sick laughter was the last thing I heard before I passed out.

When I came to the Enforcer was standing in the corner facing me, wringing wet with sweat, smoking a cigarette and contemplating his work. The whole thing had lasted less than five minutes, but he was sated; he'd done his job well. He'd inflicted the maximum amount of suffering short of death. He motioned indifferently to the guards. They untied my hands and feet, grabbed me under the arms and dragged me into the prison yard where they dumped me in a heap. Again I passed out.

It was dark and I was lying in my hut when I regained consciousness for the second time. Travis was holding my head up, coaching me to sip from a cup in his hand, and Jassy was sitting beside him, shaking his head in disgust, swearing revenge. The Filipino bastard really did a job on me. My testicles were so swollen that I couldn't move off my back or close my legs, and the hemorrhaging was extensive; red streaks criss-crossed my testicles and penis where the blood vessels had ruptured. My bladder was too sore to touch and when I pissed the pain was excruciating and my urine was bright red with blood. But there was nothing anyone could do, and I refused to be taken to the sick hut, thinking that I would recover faster in my own hut, relying instead on Travis and Jassy to bring me my rice and water until I was capable of fetching them myself. It took weeks before I could function normally, and for a long time after that I thought I'd lost my manhood. I was terribly ashamed; many months would elapse before I recovered my will to survive and to resist, before I got myself back to the place I'd been at mentally, physically, and emotionally.

One last note about that incident: not once while The Enforcer was torturing me, or in the days that followed, was I visited by any of the English officers. Not only had the Major prohibited them from sympathizing with me, or protecting me, but he had also forbidden them from making or keeping any record of what had occurred. As far as the Major was concerned, it had never happened.

No one else, though, was quite so willing to write it off. No one else was waging a personal vendetta against me, and not one Aussie doubted for a moment that the Major was to blame. They knew it never would have happened without his implicit okay, they just didn't know what to do about it.

Chapter Fourteen

With the advent of the Wets in the summer of 1943, an epidemic of colds and bronchial pneumonia spread quickly through the Hotel Tacloban, compounding our already ungovernable medical problems and sealing the fate of our worst cases. At first we were constantly protesting to Captain Yoshishito about the lack of medical supplies we were receiving from him, but by the end of the year we knew better than to waste our time and effort. Captain Yoshishito steadfastly refused our appeals to both international law and basic human decency, and complaints themselves became odious in their futility.

There was absoultely nothing we could do to combat disease. We had no medicine at all. Malaria, dysentery, yellow jaundice, beriberi, dengue fever, scurvy, pellagra, diphtheria and sickness we couldn't identify ran rampant through our ranks. We had no quinine or atabrine for malaria. No sulfur drugs for dysentery and infections. No antiseptic for cuts, gouges and puncture wounds received at work or as a result of torture. No bandages, no scalpels, no soap. Nothing. Nor was there any relief for the men who came to camp with combat wounds. One unfortunate man had a terrible shrapnel wound in the groin that oozed puss and blood for months until he developed gangrene and died. Another man arrived in camp with his knee cap blown away; when it finally healed, the leg was unbendable, the foot turned inward at an obscene ninety degree angle. There were many other similar cases.

Because we had no doctors—not even any trained medics— medical care consisted solely in what we were able to provide ourselves. In response, several compassionate men volunteered to work as orderlies in the sick hut, bringing the sick their rice and water, urging them to eat, tending to our dying with nothing more than words of comfort and consolation.

We tried to make the sick hut habitable, but to no avail—

112

sick men covered by flies and their own filth slept on defiled reed mats on the damp ground, shivering, coughing, crying out in pain. In the beginning, Captain Yoshishito would periodically send his junior officers to look in, to make sure that not one in the sick hut was malingering, but the stench in there made them nauseous and they were afraid of contagious diseases (like the Major), so eventually they stopped.

No one went willingly to the sick hut. Few returned.

The men just got sicker and sicker through the summer months, with the mortality rate climbing steadily through September, October and November, then climaxing in December when more than twenty men were confined to the sick hut with dysentery alone. Harry Barnsworth and Jeff Connelly both succumbed to dysentry that month. Harry was the first fatality in our hut. And no one stepped forward to lead our little Sunday church services after Jeff passed away (everyone was too embarassed) and we experienced a rapid decline in attendance. Those of us who continued to go tried passing the Bible around and reading our favorite passages out loud, but everyone was losing the knack of concentration, and soon the services stopped altogether.

The mood in camp was awful. We were all feeling the gut-wrenching stomach cramps of dysentery that are twenty times more painful than ordinary dry heaves, the kind that made you double over and wince when your bowels moved. Signs of vitamin deficiencies were becoming more visible, too; festering sores covered our skin, our ankles were swelling, our vision was failing, and burning feet (malnutritional neuritis) made a man's nerve endings so tender that he couldn't sleep. Beriberi and dengue fever were sapping what little strength we had to rise and "do a day," and our rations, in direct response to food shortages brought about by the naval blockade, were continually growing shorter. Out of all of us malaria victims suffered most, the hair-raising screams of delirious men issuing forth from the huts twenty-four hours a day.

One of the worst things was that no one died quickly; it was always painful and protracted and there was never an easy way out. But no one empathized too much. Too much empathy weakened a man's ability to resist and to survive, so that gradually, like doctors, we became emotionally immunized to the death and dying around us. There was even a guilt-ridden moment of relief when someone else died, a sense that fate took him, not me, therefore I must be destined to live. But it was no consolation to see our little cemetery grow and grow and eventually it seemed like every Australian hut had lost at least one man.

A death and burial was the one instance when the Aussies acted like disciplined soldiers. Although it was hard to do under the circumstances, we tried our best to make the funeral services as dignified as possible. There were a couple of things working against us. First of all, even though our cemetery had been situated where the ground was most solid, the grave detail could only dig down for a foot and-a-half, and then they hit a two-and-a-half foot layer of sand. Below that was water. There was no wood for coffins and no extra cloth for shrouds, and the bodies had to be buried within two hours, before they began to decompose. There was little time for mourning.

The Japanese expected us to cremate the bodies, as is their Shinto custom, but we wouldn't hear of it. We cleaned the body, then four men carried it forth and laid it in the hole. Then everyone stood at attention while a few words were spoken, committing the man's soul to heaven. After that there followed a moment of silence, then the Lord's Prayer, then the Brits sang, "A Mighty Fortress Is Our God":

> *A mighty fortress is our God,*
> *A bulwark never failing;*
> *Our helper he, amid the flood,*
> *Of mortal ills prevailing.*

Funerals were brief, eerie, and depressing. Death was so close to us, and we related to it so deeply, that we rushed to get away from it as quickly as we could. No one paid visits to the cemetery. That part of the Hotel Tacloban stank of noxious gases emitted from corpses rotting in shallow graves. It stank of hatred.

I sometimes wonder, now, what the military did with the remains of the men we buried there. I wonder, are they still there, or have they been moved to some military cemetry in Australia? Sometimes I think I should be buried there too.

We were all searching for something positive to hang our hopes on during the dark days of December, 1943, as Christmas was approaching, so once again we arranged to have a little pageant play. The Brits, with customary forethought, had saved the structural material from the previous year, and about a week before Christmas (no one was sure of the exact date) they began to re-assemble the stage and the principal actors began re-rehearsing their lines. A sense of community spirit, together with traces of good will toward fellow (white) men started surfacing in camp, rising above the morass of death and disease and drudgery that weighed so heavily upon us.

The strains at that particular time were worse than any before at the Hotel Tacloban. Three days before Christmas, two men died. Two days before Christmas, three men died, and two more died the following day. Most died from malaria or dysentery or a combination of the two, but we never knew why one man died. The feeling of hopelessness, amplified by our hatred of the Major (whom we blamed for many of the deaths), created so much unhappiness and so much tension between the Aussies and the Brits, that Christmas seemed to portend the end of the world, not the beginning.

And then, on Christmas Eve, 1943, completely without warning, four Australians broke out of camp! Three of them—Travis MacNaughton, Jassy Colby, and Larry Whitlam—were quartered in my hut. The fourth man, Tommy Phillips, lived in a hut diagonally across the prison yard. After that, things would never be the same at the Hotel Tacloban.

Larry left first that night, about half-an-hour after nightfall. I had no idea what was happening or why he was leaving, but my intuition (a sixth sense that's highly refined in POWs) warned me even then that something extraordinary was coming down the pike. My antennae were up when Jassy ducked out about half-an-hour later, and I was aroused and fully alert when Travis exited thirty minutes after that.

I must admit, the three of them had never before left the hut so systematically, and I had my suspicions right from the beginning. And yet the mere fact that they had left in a premeditated manner was not in itself cause for undue alarm. It wasn't *that* unusual for men to slip out at night to share cigarettes, companionship, and the coolness of night—if they were willing to take the risk. So—initially, I didn't think they were pulling off an escape. I guess I was lulled into a false sense of security by the sheer audacity of such an act. And I couldn't help noticing that they had left without carrying any equipment tied around their belts or stuffed down their shorts; I knew if they were really serious about breaking out of camp, that they would need tools for digging under the fence, and maybe even makeshift weapons. Anyway, the whole idea of escape was unimaginable. Where the hell would they go?

The why was easy enough to answer. What with men dropping like flies, they probably reasoned it out like this: "If I'm going to make it, I gotta get out of here. But I'm getting weaker every day, and I might not be strong enough to try in another month, so it's now or never!"

The where was harder to explain. North would lead them to the island of Samar, which was no different than Leyte, only that much closer to Japan. Panay, Cebu, and the South China Sea (its shipping lanes clogged with Japanese warships and merchant vessels) lay directly to the west—that way out offered little chance of success. East was the vast expanse called the Pacific Ocean, and might just as well have been 5,000 miles of desert.

Their best chance was heading south. It would mean dodging Japanese costal patrols, or penetrating into the jungle hills of Leyte and seeking refuge among guerrillas, but at least it was in the right direction—Australia. A massive manhunt would ensue in any event, and from their own experience seeing Filipino collaborationists coming into camp to help Captain Yoshishito and the Major in the management of the Hotel Tacloban, they'd have no illusions about the existence of some imaginary underground railroad manned by elements of "the resistance." Not until they got into the hills.

It seemed incredibly unlikely that they were meeting any of the local Filipinos at some prearranged time and place, although it would have been essential for them to have the knowledge and cooperation of outside contracts. As Caucasians they would stand out like raisins in rice pudding during daylight hours. They couldn't possibly travel after the sun had risen; they'd need trustworthy accomplices to hide them during the day, and reliable guides to steer them at night.

In retrospect, there is only one logical explanation I can come up with. Here it is: the four men broke out of camp, with Duff's consent, because someone they implicitly trusted was waiting outside to whisk them away. Somehow, someone connected with Allied Intelligence (a guerrilla, perhaps, contacting a Filipino double-agent posing as a collaborationist inside the camp) must have gotten a message to them with a plan and a promise that a submarine was sitting off the coast. Otherwise the idea was preposterous.

One thing is for sure: in view of the Major's nasty habit of never checking our huts at the same time on successive nights, Travis and the others had decided that an early exit afforded them the widest margin of safety. Every hour that passed, after they had left the hut, increased their chances of success.

Every hour that passed after they'd left also increased my suspicion that they had indeed escaped. I was terribly excited and I couldn't fall asleep. Christ! If they could pull it off, that meant I could do it, too. If I'd known what they were planning, I'd have made an absolute idiot of myself begging them to let me go along.

I realize now that's exactly why they never asked me to go along. That's why I was never a part to camp intrigues, and why I never knew what was going on. The Aussies insulated me from sensitive matters not only for my own protection, but also because they considered me too young, too impetuous, and too reckless to be trusted. That hurt. They thought I was crazy, but hell, wasn't escape the ultimate act of bravado?

Finally, in the wee hours of the morning after midnight, the Major, alone and at the end of his nightly rounds, stood in front of the entrance to our hut and demanded to know, "Is everyone in there awake?" From the nervous inflections in his voice, I knew something was wrong.

Bossy, Pip, Carney and I were the only ones left inside. No one stirred. No one responded.

From my mat on the ground I could barely discern the contours of the Major's form at the entrance to our hut, but as he stepped inside, I could tell from the strained impatience etched on his face that he wasn't at all surprised by the three empty mats. He knew the men were gone; he knew exactly what he wanted to say, and he couldn't wait to say it.

The Major moved deeper into the hut until he stood before my mat. I could see him clearly now as he pointed down at me and hissed, "Where are the three men who are missing? Answer me now! That's an order!"

Although the Major and I had never been on speaking terms prior to that, it was nevertheless a simple enough question for me to answer. "How the fuck should I know?," I said.

Angrily, the Major turned away from me and proceeded to ask the other men the same question, receiving, with a bit more tact, the same response from each of them. No one was talking. We weren't sure if Travis and Jassy and Larry were still in camp making preparations to leave, or if they were already outside the fence. In either case, we sure as hell weren't about to jeopardize their chances, however slim they were, by sharing our thoughts on the subject with our lovely Major. Our lovely Major, obviously, was hunting them down. It was impossible to understand *why* he would want to turn in his own men, but there he was trying to do just that.

Frustrated by our silence, realizing that we weren't about to help him out (that, on the contrary, we'd do everything in our power to delay him), the Major stepped out of the hut and stood rigidly in the darkness, trembling ever so slightly with rage. I could see the wheels spinning in his head as he ran down his list of options, contemplating his next move. There was sufficient reason for him to assume that the men were still in camp—guys often gathered at night to talk, to share cigarettes and companionship, and some men even found ways of bribing the guards out of rice wine (I'd had a swig once, but it tasted awful, its only enjoyable quality being its wetness), and there was always the possibility that they'd slipped off into a corner, knocked off a bottle of sake, then buried it.

He must be thinking along those lines, I told myself. Otherwise, why was he standing there?

Then again, maybe he wasn't. There's no way of knowing what goes on in that man's mind, I reminded myself as the Major marched off across the yard to make a second check in all the huts, on the off-chance that the missing men were still in camp. At least, that's what I assumed.

But the Major wasn't gone long enough to have conducted a thorough hut-to-hut search and he returned almost immediately with the ranking British NCO, Sgt. Major Godhall, at his side. Goodhall was a barrel-chested man about forty years old, a lifer in the English Army who, giving the devil his due, I could see was most reluctant to participate in the Major's inquisition. I think that Goodhall secretly hoped the Aussies would get away. In any case, what happened next was very odd. Through Goodhall, the Major ordered Bossy, Pip, Carney and me off our pads and outside. The moon was new and the night was charged with electricity as we stood tight-lipped at attention, waiting for the grilling to begin. Diagonally across the prison yard we could sense more than see about ten men assembled in front of Tommy's hut—that was our first hint that someone else was involved in whatever was going on.

The Major stood in front of us, subconsciously banging his fist against his hip and rocking back and forth on his feet. A muscle twitched along his jawline before he spoke, and when his words came, they were clipped and precisely ennunciated, his tenor voice rising in pitch as he asked each of us in turn, "Where are they? Tell me, damn you. I want to know now!"

But we weren't about to budge, regardless of what he said or threatened to do to us. Play dumb. Always remain inscrutable. Don't ask questions and don't volunteer answers.

119

Those are the first lessons you learn in prison. Those are the rules of the game, and there was a hell of a lot more at stake here than usual.

Our lack of cooperation infuriated the Major. His chest heaved once and he gulped for breath. "If there is something going on here..." he said slowly, sternly, trying to keep his voice from cracking.... "If these men have tried to escape...if they have, God help them...then they have broken a sacred covenant and they *will* pay dearly."

The Major paused at the point for dramatic effect, then proceeded. "If these four men have indeed escaped, then let it be known that you men will be treated as their accomplices. You too will be considered part of this rebellion, and you *will* be treated accordingly. Do I make myself clear?"

He paused again, allowing us time to reconsider. But we weren't buying it, so he pressed on. "If any one of you knows anything at all concerning the whereabouts of these men...or if any of you are in an-y-way protecting them...anyway at all!...then I will see to it personally that whatever punishment is meted out...it will apply as much to you as to them. Do you understand me?" he asked between clenched teeth, "I WILL NOT TOLERATE ANARCHY!!"

The Major's tirade made one thing perfectly clear; if nothing else, he was already convinced that the men had escaped. What wasn't quite so clear was how he knew, or why he hadn't requested the Japanese guards to conduct an extensive search of the camp, or why he hadn't notified his pal, Captain Yoshishito. His failure to look for hard physical evidence (a hole under the fence, for instance) suggested to me that someone may have informed. I began to suspect that the Major may have possessed all the relevant facts from the outset. That what we were seeing was just a charade to protect his informant.

Having made no impression on the men in my hut, the Major's next move was to order Goodhall to muster the entire camp for a head-count. Ten minutes later, everyone was assembled in the eerie pre-dawn darkness for roll call. When that'd been completed, the Major ordered the British NCOs to search each and every hut while we stood at ease, whispering softly among ourselves. By then everyone knew what had transpired. The identities of the escapees, as well as the fact of their disappearance, were now firmly established. A ripple of excitement swept through our ranks.

The Major ordered Goodhall to bring us to attention, then commenced to deliver the same speech our hut had already heard to the rest of the camp. It was an emotionally charged appeal to our collective better judgement and devotion to duty in which he stressed, in a quavering voice, that he had given his word of honor as a Gentleman and officer in the English Army—that a sacred covenant between him and Captain Yoshishito had been broken—and *that* was the issue. According to the Major, we were not acting honorably by shielding our comrades, but rather, we were doing ourselves a grave injustice. While he harangued us, he worked himself into an unbelieveable fury.

But the Australians weren't swayed. Every man there knew how easy it would have been for the bastard to look the other way, at least until morning roll call. Every man there was thinking the same thing: if just one of the Aussies could get away, our morale would soar and be sustained for months. So, even while the Major was speaking, the taunts and catcalls started coming at him from the shadowy rear ranks. Shouts of "Traitor!" and "Coward!" pierced the night like luminous tracers.

The Major stood up straighter, stiffened his upper lip and swore up and down that he only had our best interests at heart. But everyone there knew he was only out for himself. That he was afraid he'd be held responsible if the Aussies made good their escape.

"You yellow son-of-a-bitch!" someone shouted.

"Bloody traitor!" another man yelled.

With that the taunts grew louder and bolder, each one another slap in the Major's face, until he could stand no more.

"Sgt. Major," he said scornfully. "Bring these men to order."

"Ten-huh!" Goodhall bellowed, snapping to attention himself.

A moment of uncomfortable silence ensured. Let him have his say, it whispered.

"So," the Major stated flatly, "you've made your feelings known. All right then, have it your way. But listen to me now, and hear me well." He puffed up his chest. "I will not allow this unbelievable display of insubordination to go unpunished. Therefore, your Christmas pageant play is hereby cancelled. I hope you're satisfied." Then he turned once more to Goodhall and said smugly, "Sgt. Major, dismiss the troops."

"Fuck you! You English bastard!" one of the Aussies yelled.

Realizing, at last, that he was only wasting his words, the Major took the last pathetic step away from duty and human decency and reported directly to Captain Yoshishito. The bastard informed.

Chapter Fifteen

Back in our huts, the impact of what was happening struck us full force, shattering the brittle spectre of fear and self-pity which had, up until then, kept us in chains. Suddenly we had four heroes. Suddenly the adrenalin was coursing through our veins, filling us with a sense of our own latent power. We began to pace restlessly, one minute cursing the Major, his officers, his NCOs, and his Japanese cohorts, the next minute praising Travis and Jassy and Larry and Tommy. Nothing like this had ever happened before—sleeping was totally out of the question! Although Aussies are by nature loath to demonstrate exuberance, Travis and his co-conspirators had reignited the spirit of defiance within them and it spread through the Hotel Tacloban like wildfire. Beginning in one hut, overflowing into another, then another, a chorus of incited Australians released months of pent-up anger and frustration in one glorious outburst of unabashed singing. "Tipperary" and "Waltzing Matilda" filled the Hotel Tacloban, until it became a contest to see which row of huts could sing the loudest.

Meanwhile, from the moment Sgt. Major Goodhall had called the roll, Japanese guards had been gathering in the prison yard, confused and frightened by our show of strength. They knew they were sitting on top of a volcano, and that the uprising had to be squashed before it erupted totally out of control, but they were reluctant to split up into smaller groups and to advance on both sides of camp simultaneously, so they formed up into two equal groups, one of which stayed in the open while the other moved down one row of huts at a time. Squealing like stuck pigs, threatening us with their rifles and bayonets, they entered each hut, screaming at us to quiet down. But, for fear that the Aussies might stampede and maybe overrun the camp, their officers had given them orders not to shoot anyone, and no sooner would they suppress one side, than the other would start whooping and howling and carrying on all over again.

One side of camp was singing:

It's a long way to Tipperary,
It's a long way to go;
It's a long way to Tipperary,
To the sweet girl that I know!

When the Japanese advanced on them, and brought them under control, the other side started singing:

Waltzing Matilda, Waltzing Matilda,
You'll come a-waltzing Matilda with me.
And his ghost can be heard as you pass by the billabong,
"You'll come a-waltzing Matilda with me."

For once, it seemed, we had the upper hand, if only for a moment. It was the most uplifting experience we'd had in months, and my body was tingling all over from the excitement. Even the British EMs were with us; incited by four brave Aussies willing to risk it all on a single roll of the dice, they too felt the animating surge of hope in their souls.

The heckling of the Major, the British officers and NCOs and the Japanese continued for nearly an hour, as did the singing and hooting and shouts of "Coo-eee!" until the voices fell silent, replaced by apprehension and concern for the escapees. For the remainder of the night we listened intently to the sounds of light footsteps and hushed voices as the Japanese guards mobilized their forces outside our huts. Less than an hour before sunrise we heard the camp's dilapidated Model-T Ford sputter and spit as it started up. Our hearts sank when we heard it pull out of camp.

Dawn comes quickly in Leyte, striding with giants steps over the Pacific Ocean, splashing brilliant reds and golds across

* "Tipperary" written and composed by Jack Judge and Harry Williams; copyright MCMXII by B. Feldman and Co., London. "Waltzing Matilda" written and composed by A.B. Patterson.

124

the sky, bursting on the scene. And then, as quickly as it comes, it settles down under an oppressive veil of heat and humidity. So, too, the tumult of the previous night ran its course and subsided. We met the day with muted anticipation.

At daybreak on Christmas morning, 1943, Travis, Jassy, Larry and Tommy were brought back to the Hotel Tacloban, badly beaten, blindfolded and bound in chains on the back of the camp's flat-bed Ford. The Japanese parked in the center of the prison yard, guards hastily surrounding the truck. We were ordered out of our huts and assembled in a tight arc four or five men deep, facing our officers, with no uniformity and no assigned places other than with our NCOs up front. Although I purposefully stood at the rear of the formation, trying to evaporate into the crowd, no more than ten yards separated me from our defeated, anguished officers.

Duff and Jerry and Carroll stood behind the Major to his right, and the British officers took their places behind him to his left. Flanking the Major, his chalk-white face as cold as ice, Sgt. Major Goodhall aimed his hard eyes at some imaginary point beyond the barbed wire. The mood in camp had plummeted from euphoria to deep despair.

Heavily-armed Japanese guards were stationed everywhere throughout the camp compound, their rifles trained on us, their machine gun squads set-up in enfilading positions around our compact formation. It was the first time I'd seen the entire Japanese contingent assembled at once. It was also the first time I'd seen Duff so visibly shaken or so powerless in the face of disaster. A sense of dread, of impending doom, hung suspended in the heavy tropical air as Sgt. Major Goodhall brought us to attention. On orders from the Japanese, a detail of Aussies was sent to the infirmary to carry out our sick and to hold them up in line. No one was to be spared the executions.

When everyone was present, Captain Yoshishito advanced and stood impassively beside the Major, both of their backs turned indifferently on the open space separating them from the four condemned Aussies on the back of the truck. With Yoshishito was the Executioner, a scabbard hanging from his hip, its tip dragging along the ground, the handle on the ceremonial sword itself almost a foot long and tucked up under his arm. Expressionless, their hooded eyes darting left and right, Yoshishito's lieutenants stood poised and alert in front of Travis, Jassy, Larry and Tommy.

Through Goodhall, the Major ordered Duff to join him and Captain Yoshishito.

Duff refused. He didn't move a muscle, he just stood there with his hands clenched in fists at his sides and his lips drawn taut.

The Major personally ordered Duff to the spot.

Again Duff refused.

I have no way of knowing what his thoughts were at that moment, but I do know this: Duff was more than just a man, he was a symbol—our battle flag—and without him we were lost. What happened to Duff was more important to us than what happened to any other individual or group, and if the Major had made the Japanese take any sort of physical action against him, it would have been rebellion for sure. The Major knew that, too, but Duff's public defiance was just one more slap in his face, just one more blow to his monumental ego. He had to do something. So, struggling to control his anger, the Major proceeded to strip Duff of his commission, then swore to God that he'd have him court-martialed for disobeying orders.

Meanwhile, everyone knew what was about to befall the four men on the back of the truck, and everyone looked to Duff. The moment of truth had arrived; it was up to him, and to him alone, to decide whether or not we would rush the guards. It was our duty to obey.

Maybe it was because we had not sharpened sticks into knives or spears; because we had no clubs to swing or stones to throw; because it was rifles and machine guns against unarmed men. Maybe Travis and the others had squared it with Duff before they'd escaped and had agreed that there was nothing he could do to save them, if they were caught. Or maybe it was simply a case of Duff having weighed the lives of four men against the lives of over one hundred. He was standing close enough to me so that I could see the tears streaming down his face.

Captain Yoshishito nodded curtly to his lieutenants, who

in turn ordered the guards to pull the four bedraggled men off the truck and into the open space between it and us. Tommy was reacting the worst; he'd gone completely to pieces. He was crying hysterically and had to be dragged kicking and screaming by the guards. Jassy and Larry were sobbing to themselves, struggling hard not to collapse. Travis was the only man who had not broken down. Standing ramrod straight, no sign of fear visible on his bearded face, he calmly asked that his blindfold be removed. The Major, with Captain Yoshishito's approval, granted Travis's request, and one of the Japanese officers untied it and pulled it off. And even though he stared directly into the rising sun, Travis didn't blink. His eyes were glowing fiery red.

The guards separated the men four paces apart. They motioned for Travis to kneel in the dust with his head bent forward and he did so, without hesitation. The Executioner drew his sword and moved beside him. Dawn cast long shadows across the prison yard—the moment seemed arrested by the level sun.

I wanted to look away as I watched over the shoulder of the man standing in front of me, but there was some crazy compulsion to see. Try as I might, I couldn't move my eyes from the blade on the ceremonial sword, which was long and slightly curved, but neither heavy nor thick nor ornate. Both hands on the hilt, the Executioner raised it above his shoulder, the sunlight momentarily glinting off the steel, then he brought it down.

I closed my eyes when he hit Travis—I couldn't watch anymore after that—I just stook there with my eyes shut tight, hating myself and shivering inside, wanting desperately to cover my ears with my hands. But that wasn't allowed, and three more times I heard that awful sound (the little bastards saved Tommy for last, for the devastating psychological effect), and then there was silence. Merciful silence. And in that absence of sound that followed the beheadings of Travis MacNaughton, Justice Colby, Larry Whitelam, and Tommy Philips, there wasn't one man, Brit or Aussie, who didn't know deep in his heart that the Major had to go. Speaking for every man there, Sgt. Major Goodhall, good soldier of the disgraced English Army, a man who'd been turned inside-out by his commanding officer's treachery, a man who could no longer stand idly by while his honorable world crumbled around him, with utter contempt, turned and spit in the Major's face.

Stunned speechless, his eyes blinking rapidly and his jaw muscle twitching uncontrolably, the Major quickly wiped the spittle away, then proceeded to strip Goodhall of his rank and ordered him placed under arrest. "Was there to be no end to the insults heaped upon him?" he seemed to be thinking. The man was insane.

Captain Yoshishito was astounded. It was inconceivable to him that ordinary soldiers of any army would demonstrate even the slightest hint of disrespect to their commanding officer. Such acts of defiance ate away at the very foundation upon which the chain of command is structured. Yoshishito stood there bewildered, regarding the situation with total disbelief—genuinely grieved that his brother officer, our lovely Major, had once again been publicly disgraced. Regaining his senses, Captain Yoshishito quickly signalled to his lieutenants, who selected eight Australians at random to dig graves and bury the dead. Then, speaking through a Filipino interpretor, he notified us that we were to be denied the right to conduct funeral services, that there would be no general issue of rice for the next two days, and that only the minimum water ration would be distributed, British officers excluded. The Australian officers were offered the same exemption, but flatly turned it down.

No one waited to be dismissed. Everyone just turned around and walked back to their huts.

Chapter Sixteen

Outrage over the beheadings was unanimous, and it was agreed that the Major must be eliminated if we were to survive. Thus, with the expressed consent of every Australian EM in camp, three of the most highly respected men organized a war council composed of a spokesman from each hut which met that same night in a hut belonging to several of the older men. At this meeting, deliberations were short and to the point, it being decided that the Major must be murdered within forty-eight hours, before he betrayed one more man, and in such a manner that it would be apparent to the Japanese that we had done it. Garroting was chosen as the method best suited to this purpose, and as the most practical, and a team of three men was deemed necessary to carry out the task. But the risks involved were enormous, and when the war council called for volunteers, no one stepped forth.

Subsequently, over eighty Aussies agreed to draw straws to determine who'd do the job, with the same three men who'd organized the war council moving cautiously through camp on the following morning, providing each willing man with a chance to test his luck. There were three short straws in a fistful, and I drew the first one. The next four men to pull short straws backed down, two on moral grounds, saying they couldn't kill in cold blood, the other two admitting they were afraid. Ultimately, the task fell to me, Sergeant Toby Donaldson and Ned Courtney, two hard-bitten Aussies for whom revenge was neither a crime nor a risk, but a duty.

On the evening of December 26, 1943, the three of us met in Donaldson's hut, which was adjacent to the British EMs hut on the south side of camp, and thus the Australian outpost closest to the Major's quarters. Donaldson's hutmates, on his orders, had vacated the premises, dispersing to other huts while we formulated our plan of action in seclusion. We knew we'd only get one crack at it, and there was a great deal of pressure to act fast, before the Brits accidentally stumbled on our plot. Or were informed.

The first thing we had to take into consideration, as we huddled together in the darkness, whispering conspiratorially, was that the executions had made the Japanese guards more jittery than usual. Under "normal" conditions they were wary of the menacing, surly Australians, keeping their distance and entering our huts only to break-up fist fights, but whenever an Aussie died, for whatever reason, they receded nervously into the background, fearful of reprisals. Therefore we based our plan on the supposition that the guards, true to form, would be watching the fence and the main gate that night, but not the huts.

Meanwhile, Duff was inadvertently setting the stage for our sortie. To insure that they would maintain their authority, by virtue of non-complicity, should we fail to accomplish our mission, neither Duff nor Jerry nor Carroll had been told of our intentions. However, it would be misleading to say that Duff was unaware of the cry for blood; Duff knew better than anyone that the Australians were on the verge of over-running the Hotel Tacloban, and while we were mapping out our strategy, he was taking steps of his own to keep the lid from blowing. We simply coordinated out plans with his.

In an effort to forestall an outright revolt, which could only lead to our self-destruction, Duff had invited the British junior officers to his hut to discuss what measures should be taken against the Major. The Brit delegation, headed by Lieutenant Downey, was acutely aware that the Major had finally gone too far in his collaboration with the enemy. The mere fact that he felt justified in betraying four men under his care—that he felt no remorse at having sentenced them to death—convinced the Brits once and for all that the Major had lost his sense of proportion, and with it his ability to command. In addition, they too recognized the vengeful mood of the Australians, and they were willing to seek a compromise solution, if only to ensure the safety of their own troops.

Granted, the Brits were intelligent enough to realize that Duff, more than anybody, was in no position to confront the Major with his treachery, and they also realized that the responsibility for restraining the Major was theirs, but, when all was said and done, it was a dilemma they were critically ill-equipped to handle. By training and tradition, the Brits were totally unaccustomed to independent action of any sort. Although Duff sought to assure them that, in a situation like the one facing them now, they not only had the right, but they also had a *duty*, to relieve an incompetent officer of his command, they were nevertheless paralyzed by doubts. It didn't matter to Downey or the others that the Major was demented and a mortal threat to everyone in camp; in the final analysis, mutiny for the British junior officers was unthinkable.

All the time Duff was arguing his case, Donaldson, Courtney and I were embarking on a more decisive course of action. For us there was no turning back. Once we had decided that the Japanese guards presented no real problem, as long as we steered clear of the fence, we next had to decide how to get past the one hut on the south side of camp occupied by British EMs, without being noticed. That was our major challenge. We knew that once we'd worked our way beyond that hut, we could hide in relative safety behind the empty British junior officer's hut. The choice was how to get by. We could either use stealth while approaching our objective, sneaking by one-by-one, or else we could walk nonchalantly through the center of camp, which, if we had the bad luck to be spotted, would arouse less suspicion and might be easier to talk our way out of. We decided on the latter, along with the excuse that we were looking for Lieutenant Downey, just in case we were questioned. We also agreed that Donaldson would enter through the yard entrance, while Ned and I rushed in from the rear.

Finally, we had to decide what to do once we were inside the Major's hut, and that's the part that bothered me. Despite everything I'd been through, in New Guinea as well as at the Hotel Tacloban, there was still no blood on my hands. To my knowledge I hadn't killed a single Japanese, and yet here I was setting off to murder an English Major. Wasn't it a repudiation of everything I believe in? I'd been an Eagle Scout.

I felt good saluting the colors, reciting "The Pledge Of Allegiance," singing "America The Beautiful." My only intention in joining the army had been to help bring the war to a hasty conclusion, but somewhere along the line, everything had been turned around. The only thing that hadn't changed was the way I felt inside.

Luckily for me, Donaldson and Courtney were mature men in their thirties, men who were mentally tougher than I, men who had the strength of will to fix on the job at hand and follow it through to the end, whatever the consequences. They liked me, and they knew it wasn't fear of dying that caused my distress, so, much to my relief, they offered to do the actual garroting while I served as lookout. After that, there was nothing more to say.

We sat in silence in Donaldson's hut until we saw the British junior officers pass us on their way to Duff's, then we waited, postponing our move for as long as we dared, for as long as our nerves could hold out. Timing was everything. We wanted to delay long enough to allow the Major to fall asleep, but not so long that the Brits returned before we'd done the deed. We were counting on Duff to keep them occupied for a few hours, but there was not way of knowing just how long that would be. A lot depended on luck.

It was around midnight when Donaldson said the time was right; we shook hands then walked together into the stillness of the prison yard, turned west toward the Japanese barracks, nothing but empty space and darkness between them and us. I was never more alert than I was at that moment. Being very careful to check around to make sure we weren't noticed, we strolled casually passed the British EMs hut until we drew abreast of the British junior officers' hut, at which point we veered sharply south, slipping unseen into the shadows. We paused one last time, listening intently, holding our breath. Every nerve in my body was taut.

No sounds of stirring came from within the Major's hut, but, none of us ever having been inside his quarters, we were unaware of the layout, as well as his sleeping habits, and we wondered whether he was on a mat or a cot. There was only one way to find out. Donaldson motioned that it was time to go. We separated, Courtney and I edging our way around the rear of the hut, Donaldson entering simultaneously from the front.

Major Cumyns was asleep on his back on a floor mat, the little starlight that penetrated the darkness illuminating his face with satin serenity. Donaldson crept toward the unsuspecting form on tiptoe, quickly, silently, in his hands a leather cord, the type that binds the handle on an officer's revolver to his holster. He knelt before the Major's head while Courtney, who'd entered before me, straddled the Major's body, sat down pressing his knees together, stuffed a rag in the Major's mouth, all in one movement. Awakened, the Major's head snapped up high enough for Donaldson to loop the cord around his neck—only then, as Courtney pressed his scrawny chest to the gound and Donaldson tightened the noose with all his might, did the Major realize that he was being murdered by Australians. Squirming frantically, he tried to wedge his legs under Courtney's weight. His hands clutched at Courtney's arms, then at the garrot, then froze halfway between in mid-air. Then they fell limply to the floor.

I crouched at the front entrance, peering into the prison yard abyss, my ears pricked-up for the slightest sound. Behind me, Donaldson and Courtney waited until they were certain that the Major was dead, then we retreated to the shadows of the British junior officers' hut, caught our breath, stilled our hearts, then returned, the same way we'd come, to Donaldson's hut. There we collected our wits and split up, Courtney and I going back to our own huts. The plan had gone off without a hitch, except, maybe, for one small thing—the sound of the Major's pathetic gurgling and choking would haunt me for the rest of my days.

Corporal Trimbly, the Major's lackey, discovered his master's body early the following morning. Shocked and badly frightened, he reported directly to Lieutenant Downey, now the ranking POW in the Hotel Tacloban. Downey, who'd returned from his discussion with Duff uninspired to action,

133

felt as though he been tricked, deceived, betrayed. But, as usual, he didn't quite know how to react.

Once Captain Yoshishito had officially appointed him Acting POW Camp Commandant, Downey stepped reluctantly into the Major's shoes, pursuing his leadership role with a lot less enthusiasm than his predecessor. He had learned his lesson well. It had been established beyond any doubt that the price of collaboration was as high as failed escape, and in that sense the assasination had accomplished its primary goal; the main source of pressure upon us, Major Cumyns, had been effectively removed, and we'd assumed a greater measure of control over our fate. "The Book," unfortunately, remained in British hands.

In sharp contrast to their wishy-washy officers, the British EMs felt that what had been done to the Major was tantamount to a declaration of war, a reckless act which had needlessly endangered everyone in camp. Animosity between them and the Aussies climbed to a new level of intensity, and from that day on the Brits closed ranks, never again trusting nor associating with us. Never again would there be any fraternizing on the chow line; if the Aussies arrived first, the Brits hung back en masse and waited until the Aussies were done. And vice versa. From that day on the British EMs lived in perpetual fear of the Aussies; they were so shook-up, in fact, that they buried the Major's body at night, surreptiously, in a far corner of our little cemetry which is forever England's. Even our Sunday church services stopped altogether, from that fateful day on, whatever sense of community that may have existed having been buried along with the Major.

Not surprisingly, the Aussies didn't give a good goddamn; in their opinion it was better to be feared, by the Brits as well as by the Japanese, as a deadly force to be reckoned with, rather than being taken for granted. Survival was the name of the game, and if taking the law into their hands was what it took to stay alive, then that's exactly what they'd do. For too long they'd suffered under the Major's tyranny, and now that the tables had been turned, now that the Major was no longer there to wheel and deal, it was just too bad if the Brits stopped receiving preferential treatment and started feeling the heat. As far as the Aussies were concerned, the new arrangement was just fine.

Although we expected that Captain Yoshishito would react violently at the loss of his right-hand man, we were pleasantly surprised at the perfunctory investigation that did ensue. Hut-to-hut interrogations were conducted by Yoshishito, his staff, and a Filipino interpretor (who understood English well enough, but spoke little Japanese). Questions were directed at the men in each hut as a group, not as individuals. And so, once again, the language barrier worked to our advantage, this time proving to be the major impediment to a successful Japanese investigation. Even though every Australian in camp knew who the principals were, not one shred of incriminating evidence was ever uncovered, nor was any damning testimony ever received. The Brits were never questioned.

We got the feeling that Captain Yoshishito was just going through the motions. It seemed to us that he really didn't care, that he too was imprisoned by the tropical intertia and overwhelming sense of futility that had held us all in thrall. Or perhaps he despised us too much to even bother prosecuting a scapegoat. In any case, no one was ever accused or singled-out for punishment. There were increased acts of cruelty on the part of the Japanese guards, and our rice ration was substantially reduced, which resulted in more medical problems, but we no longer had a traitor in our midst, and with that pressure gone, we felt we'd come out on top of the deal.

Postscript: to this day I fail whenever I try to justify my role in the Major's murder. As I've grown older and considered the factors involved—the pressure we were under and the quality of the Major in particular—I'm sure that somehow we could have circumvented the problem, rather than doing what we did. I look back and wish, as I did then, that the Major could have been persuaded to apply the same diligence in resisting the Japanese as he applied in assisting them. I wish he could have put aside his stupid prejudices and seen how determined the Aussies were to do the right thing. But he didn't. As much as he was a victim of his own compelling fear, the Major was a casualty of a culture that puts precedence on a man's position within the caste system and not on his character, where it belongs. Men like Major Cumyns, like Greek tragic heroes, are blind to their limitations, blind to their flaws. They summon disaster upon themselves.

I know that now, but I didn't know that then, and I grew to become troubled by what I had done. Not at first. At first I felt exhilarated—I felt that finally I had done something to justify my existence. But then my conscience started acting up. So, a few weeks later, after the dust had settled, I went to see Duff (who had disappeared into his hut immediately following the executions and had surfaced again only after the Major had been planted) and told him how I felt. Duff tried to put my mind at ease; he told me quite frankly that the Major had gotten exactly what he deserved, and that no one would ever blame me for what had happened. Then he went on to explain that even the English Army had no use for officers like the Major, and that any English officer who disgraces himself in the line of duty has his name scratched from the rolls of his regiment and a black mark put in its place in a ritual ceremony called, "The Degree of the White Feather." It is an ancient tradition based on cock fighting—when a cock gives up in a fight it turns its back and shows its white underplumage. If the disgraced officer is still alive, a messenger delivers the white feather to him personally, indicating that the ceremony has been performed. If he is dead, the feather is sent to his family. Duff explained that most English officers would rather die than disgrace themselves, their regiment, and their family, but that a small percentage were destined to be cowards. "You see," Duff said, "they're already dead inside."

Indeed, my actions in regard to the Major's murder pall in significance when compared to my inaction on the day Travis, Jassy, Larry, and Tommy were beheaded by the Japanese. That event instilled in me an anguish so profound and so abiding that I have lived in torment even since. I try to block out the memory, but I fail. I sleep and I dream. And when I relive that Christmas morning, I succumb to overwhelming guilt and despair. My one regret in life is that we did not rush those Japanese bastards, regardless of how many of us were killed in the process. I cannot believe that we just stood there and watched.

Chapter Seventeen

Numbness is the word that best described the state of mind at the Hotel Tacloban in 1944, the third and final phase of our imprisonment. Many men caved in after the failed escape attempt and the beheadings, and few men bothered keeping up a show of good spirits anymore. Rather, they retreated further within themselves, bracing for the hardships sure to come, desensitizing themselves to the horror and persecution surrounding them.

Notably, most of us alive at the beginning of the year would make it through, the weakest men having perished during the dysentery epidemic of 1943, and the mortality rate actually declined in 1944. From there on in we averaged one death per month, including three Aussies to executions; two men were beheaded for attacking guards while inside the camp compound, and one man was beaten to death after swinging a shovel at a guard who refused to give him water on a work detail. Work details themselves gradually diminished in size as every day more and more men collapsed from exhaustion, disease and malnutrition. It reached the point where work was scheduled on a rotating basis, but even that system proved ineffective and the Japanese guards eventually resorted to lining us up in the morning and picking out the healthy-looking ones for work that day.

The Japanese reinforcement of Leyte, which had been launched in December, 1943, resulted in even further reductions in our food supply, so that by the start of 1944 we were receiving only half a bowl of rice twice each day, with no more scraps of chicken or fish to be found. Outward signs of defiance diminished in direct proportion to decreases in our rations, and yet our determination to stand together against our oppressors persisted, percolating below our surface passivity. In fact, as we wore down physically and mentally, the spiritual bond between us actually grew stronger, and even though each man took special care to look out for himself, when it came down to the nitty-gritty the Aussies shared everything. It wasn't the sort of things that was talked about (words, if they existed, would have been inadequate to express our feelings toward one another), but it was accepted that if a man was going into or coming out of a malaria seizure, or some other medical problem, that he got the easier job.

In their dark, unfathomable way, the Japanese recognized this, and they sought to break our will to stand together, to resist them, by escalating the frequency and severity of abuse inflicted on us individually. In return, our hatred for them knew no bounds—it helped to sustain us and it helped us to bear our punishment with granite stoicism. As more and more men were beaten and tortured and killed, we looked around and knew that anyone of us could be next. There was a feeling that nothing was to be lost by dying simply to defy the little bastards—a sense of camaraderie that fueled my defiance and gave rise in me to uncontrollable urges to challenge our tormentors.

There was a second reason for my recklessness (or death wish, as it's sometimes called), and that was the extreme despondency induced by cerebral malaria. Malaria was causing me terrible fits and there were periods lasting two or three days when delirium would drive me completely out of my mind, when I couldn't recall anything that had happened, when I'd awaken in the sick hut, sweating and screaming, surrounded by moaning men and foul odors, confused as to where I was and how I'd gotten there. I was plagued by hallucinations and nightmares about Bobby and Travis and Jassy and all the other men I'd seen destroyed. Every night when I closed my eyes, I saw the faces of the men who were with me on the ambushed patrol. Believe me, it's not so hard to court death when you feel you have no right to be alive, when you view it as a welcome release.

The Hotel Tacloban was a psychological mine field where you learned to pick your way carefully through your thoughts, being sure to avoid dangerous ideas, false hopes and memories of better times. I sought out neutral turf in my quest for oblivion, but that wasn't always possible; sometimes my thoughts would drift back accidentally to my childhood and sometimes I would imagine myself sitting on a street corner in Pleasantville eating an ice-cream cone. Such thoughts only depressed me. Only by clearing my mind of all thoughts could I live from moment to moment unencumbered by distressing emotions. There was an on-going battle to block out the past and the future, and therein lay the secret to staying sane. You learned to walk the tightrope between reality and fantasy, for, if you stepped off, the hunger and anguish returned.

POWs are front line soldiers who've been cut off from supply and communication lines, at a point beyond the medics. They're surrounded by the enemy, and at the same time they have no weapons with which to defend themselves. They're trapped in a finite world where random suffering ricochets off barbed wire. A consuming rage eats away inside them.

By June of 1944, Leyte was in the throes of a famine brought about in part by a tenfold increase in the number of Japanese troops garrisoned in the island, and in part because of the US Naval blockade. All Japanese vessels, including transports loaded with Allied POWs being evacuated to mainland Japan, were potential targets for American submarines. It was the misfortune of hundreds of inmates of Davao Penal Colony to be killed when their ship was torpedoed off the southern coast of Luzon in the summer of 1944. By the end of the war, over 5,000 Allied POWs had met the same fate.

The Naval blockade was very effective, and because of it, by June we were receiving merely half a bowl of rice (about four ounces) once each day in mid-afternoon.

I also received the treatment from the Enforcer for the second time in June. A small group of us were working on the cowpath, widening it and installing culverts in preparation for the Wets, when one of the Aussies cracked a joke and I laughed, which annoyed one of the guards. Our guards were notoriously paranoid and this one probably thought I was making fun of him, so he jabbed me between the shoulder blades with his bayonet. Reflexes got the better of me—I spun around, grimaced, and made a threatening gesture at the little creep, which was a serious enough offense to warrant another session with the Enforcer. But it wasn't as bad the second time around—pain alone cannot kill a resolute man, and at least that time I knew I could survive.

Nevertheless, I was unable to walk by myself after that, and I spent the final months at the Hotel Tacloban lying inertly on my mat. My memories of those last few months are fuzzy and vague, as if I observed the world from a mental state bordering on the comatose. Indeed, there were instances when I slipped across the line. I spent June and July watching the speckled shafts of sunlight that filtered down through the faded gold fronds in my hut, or else I let my thoughts float on the heat waves pulsating outside in the prison yard. The white dust swirled in tiny tornadoes on the wind and carried me into sweet unconsciousness.

Then the Wets were with us and I was always chilled. Storm clouds gathered and darkened the sky, turning purple and violet when the lightning flashed. Rain water glistened on the level ground and rain drops splashed metronomically on the thin layer of water that had nowhere to run. Waves of rain blew into the hut, dissolving my thoughts, and time stood infinitely still. Waves of anguish rose in my gut and stuck in my throat, each successive swell of despair swamping my soul and causing me physical pain.

There were only four of us left in the hut by then, and, like good soldiers everywhere, we were very superstitious. No one in camp dared to change huts or move his pad. "I've survived so far in this spot, and I'd better not tempt fate by moving now," the reasoning went.

Interestingly enough, Pip and I—the oldest and the youngest—paired off to help one another to the chow line and to the latrine. Our coordinated movements were mechanical, geared for economy of effort. I held him up while he squatted over the slit trench, then we switched positions. When it was time to eat, it took every ounce of will power and physical strength to rise from my mat, to walk with Pip to the mess, then to extend my arm so my bowl could be half filled with rice.

Walking back to our hut, leaning on Pip for support, I

looked inside the huts and saw naked men with less energy than a leaf or a fly lying listlessly on their pads and staring vacantly into space, their deep-set eyes void of awareness. They all measured their lives in grains of rice. They all looked transparent, like skeletons wrapped in cellophane, like emaciated apparitions in some macabre carnival of the absurd. If the sunshine struck their heads they fainted. They would shiver when a rain drop landed on a shoulder. But they found a way to endure.

Back in my hut I would drift in and out of consciousness and remember what Duff once said: "You've got to hang on to your life."

How to do that? Where to find hope?

At dusk the sun would settle in between the peaks of the blue-green hills in the west. Those amorphous hills at twilight reminded me of home. Home. I imagined myself beyond the barbed wire, beyond the bamboo. I imagined the world blanketed in snow and ice. Clean and cold. The way I loved it. Back home.

1944 was a much better year for General Douglas MacArthur than it was for us. Briefly: Saidor fell in January; Hollandia, Aitape, Madang, and Alexishafen in April; Arare, Wakde, and Biak Islands in May; Noemfoor Island and Sansapor in July; and Morotai in the Moluccas in September. New Guinea was finally his and by late September he was ready to strike at the Philippines. From the moment he had fled Corregidor in March, 1942, he's been perfecting his invasion plans, and now he had amassed more than 150,000 soldiers and over 700 ships (including aircraft carriers, battleships, Destroyers, transports, cruisers and landing craft) for what was to be the biggest amphibious operation in the Pacific theatre. Not only was it to be the body blow to the Japanese Empire, it was also the avenging battle every general yearns for, the crowning achievement of MacArthur's long and distinguished career.

MacArthur's original intention was to stage a landing at Sarangani Bay, at the southern tip of Mindanao, in mid-November. But, when Naval pilots, on bombing raids conducted by Admiral "Bull" Halsey's 3rd Fleet in September, met only feeble resistance throughout the Central Philippines, MacArthur boldly opted to bypass Mindanao altogether, and to strike with everything he had at Leyte. The reason was simple enough: Leyte had the Cataisan Airstrip, Mindanao did not. Furthermore, this change in plans not only put his ground forces several hundred miles closer to mainland Japan, as well as guaranteeing them air support, but the ground work for an invasion had already been laid in Leyte. Several well-placed guerrilla radio stations were in full operation, and guerrilla chieftans united under Colonel Kangleon had stopped bickering long enough to assist various Allied Intelligence agents gathering information on Japanese coastal fortifications and defenses, troop strengths and placements. In addition, American submarines had been depositing arms, ammunition and equipment to Filipinos in Leyte since early summer, 1944, in preparation for the final assault.

As word of the impending invasion spread from barrio to barrio, morale among the Filipinos skyrocketed. In the meantime, the 15,000 newly arrived Japanese soldiers of the 16th Division (commanded by Lt. Gen. Shiro Makino) consumed vast quantities of sake as a bracer for the forthcoming shock.

In early September we began to spot squadrons of bombers flying north over the Hotel Tacloban, and we deduced, correctly, that the war was swinging against the Japanese. When Cataisan Airstrip was bombed in the middle of the month, we began to speculate that someone "out there" might know of our existence. The brown-frocked monks who for months had been gloomy, suddenly seemed jovial and winked when they passed by camp. Although they were not allowed near enough to speak to us, they smiled and with their hands held down at their sides, flashed "V" for victory with their fingers. By the beginning of October they walked with a bounce and waved to us when the guards weren't looking. We got the message that help was on the way, and we took heart, but we never imagined that tens of thousands of American soldiers would soon be storming ashore less than ten miles away.

This was a suspenseful time for us. Now that there was

chance of being rescued we found it hard to keep our excitement under wraps. Now that we had something to lose, we did not want to provoke the guards, who had become very edgy—so edgy in fact that we were afraid to cluster together. Pessimistic to the core and fearful of irrational Japanese vengeance, we wondered if we'd be massacred at night in our huts, or lined up in the prison yard and mowed down. We wondered if anyone would live to tell our story.

Some of the men wanted to take the offensive there and then, before the guards got to us, but Duff convinced them to wait. Moving casually from man to man, from hut to hut, asking everyone to hold tight, Duff contended that we weren't in any better shape to overrun the camp now than we were a few months earlier. He was absolutely right.

On October 18, 1944, advance units of the Sixth Army, in conjunction with elements of the First Cavalry Division, seized Homonhon, Suluan and Digaget Islands at the mouth of Leyte gulf, where they erected habor lights to guide the massive invasion fleet. Mine sweepers and underwater demolition teams cleared the reefless, phosphorescent waters off Leyte's northeastern coast. The hour of our deliverance was at hand.

The Camp was deserted, the Japanese gone, when we awoke at dawn on the morning of October 20 to the rumble of distant guns. Battleships were pounding the beaches prior to the landing, the ground trembled from the barrage, and some men feared that we might be shelled by our own forces. The skies to the south and east were filling up with planes, columns of yellow smoke, and white puffy clouds from ack-ack fire.

The mood in camp ranged from cautious optimism to downright panic, so we organized an impromptu discussion in the center of camp, with the able helping the sick to attend. The men who feared we might be shelled by our own forces wanted to disband and head out into the hills in small groups, but the cooler heads, led by Duff, decided that we should stay together and wait for help to come to us.

We didn't have long to wait; Army Intelligence knew we were there. Around noon, a team of highly trained Army commandos known as Rangers, backed up by a team of 1st Cavalry medics, entered the Hotel Tacloban, quickly spread out through camp and started searching in our huts, almost as though they were looking for someone in particular. They were greeted by men too weak, too overcome by bittersweet emotions—by both embarrassment and joy—to celebrate their arrival. Filthy men with long matted hair and scraggly beards; naked men covered with lice and scabs and running sores; men whose entire anatomy was visible beneath a veil of yellow-tinged skin; crippled men, some missing eyes and ears, fingers and toes; deformed men with elephantiasis and dengue fever, their grotesque movements a poor pantomine of humanity; and men with terminal illnesses for whom the Rangers' appearance meant only that help had come too late.

We couldn't understand why so many of the combat hardened Rangers had tears in their eyes. We didn't realize, at first, that they were shocked beyond words at the horror of our condition, at the monstrous degradation we'd been subjected to. They'd never seen anything like it, not in two years of war, and some of them looked away, trying to hide their revulsion. They seemed afraid that our disease, or maybe our guilt, might somehow rub off on them, and we knew they didn't want to touch us. All of them were overwhelmed by the stench, that most offensive of sensations to assault them. I could hear them talking about it with disgust, wondering out loud how we would stand it. I know I'll never smell anything like it again. Never. For over two years, between 120 (the number of men who survived) and 160 men had lived in confined quarters in a chronic state of diarrhea in a sultry climate. You just can't imagine what that smells like.

Feelings of relief at being rescued and pride at having survived without submitting to our oppressors clashed with feelings of shame at my ghastly appearance and bitterness over the countless humiliations it emphasized. I found myself suspecting a trick, like the poor man who's won the million dollar lottery, but who has yet to be paid. The change had come too fast. It didn't quite register. Was it a dream? Was it finally over? Were we really free?

Even then, I knew it wasn't true. I knew our "liberators"

could never free us from the walls we'd built around ourselves. They could never give us back the wasted years. They could never even the score.

Medical teams from the 1st Cavalry immediately began treating our worst cases, while sympathetic Rangers handed out American cigarettes, the store-bought kind with familiar names like Lucky Strike, Chesterfield, and Camel. Toothless POWs with bulging foreheads and hollow temples remembered how to smile, and spellbound Rangers staring at our little cemetery, at the shallow graves and the sea of wooden markers, wept openly. Time, which had ground to a halt, took a quantum leap forward and left me breathless in the lurch.

In the mass confusion of our "liberation," I was approached by a squad of serious-minded Rangers, was asked my name, and gave it to them. The commanding officer checked it off a list on a clipboard in his hand, then ordered me loaded onto a stretcher (I could barely crawl at that point) and separated from the Australians. Feeling like a side of beef being shipped to market, but too excited to protest, I was carried across the prison yard and shoved into the back of a canvas-covered ambulance called a six-by-six. No one seemed to notice, there was too much going on. I propped myself up on one elbow to take a look at the spectacle, and a wave of sentimentality swept through me, bringing tears to my eyes—when compared to the fully-clothed, well-fed Rangers, my comrades looked like the life had been squeezed out of them. Those who could were limping around asking questions about the war or whatever, while those who were immobile gratefully received dressings for their wounds and medicine for their sicknesses. As much as I hated the Hotel Tacloban, I loved my comrades dearly and I didn't want to leave them like this, without exchanging addresses or making arrangements to meet, without first saying goodbye, at least.

Before I had a chance to realize what was happening, two medics climbed into the rear of the six-by-six with me, and two more got into the front and started it up. I was the only POW in the vehicle, which didn't seem right, so I asked

146

permission to speak with Duff before we left. I began to grow suspicious when they refused.

"Where's Duff?" I asked. "Why won't you let me speak to him?"

"You'll see him later," they reassured me. "You'll see everyone later on. But, for the time being, we just want to get you back to someplace safe where we can take care of you. You're a very sick fellow."

Reluctantly, knowing it was a mistake I'd live to regret, I allowed myself the luxury of believing them. But that would be the last time I saw my Australian comrades or the Hotel Tacloban. The last man in, I was also the first one out.

We drove northeast along the cowpath called Highway 1 until we reached the coast, at which point the road cut back and headed straight for Tacloban. We followed it around the outer edge of the city, where groups of American GIs were posted along the wharfs, distributing canned food to the jubilant Filipinos.

"Will ya look at them animals," one of the medics remarked. The Filipinos were going nuts over the food.

"Hey!" the other guy said reproachfully. "If you was as hungry as them you'd be doing it too."

For some reason their conversation annoyed me. If they only knew how much worse it could get, then maybe they wouldn't be so goddamned sanctimonious, I thought to myself.

"Where're you guys from?" I asked, changing the subject.

"Came up from Hollandia," they replied.

I didn't recognize the name, although they seemed to take it for granted that I should, and that made me recall something Duff had once said about what I should and shouldn't expect after we were rescued. "The closer you get to civilization," he warned me, "the less people will want to hear about this. They won't be able to relate to the experience, and they won't want to know."

He was right on the money as usual. I couldn't begin to understand how the world had changed, not yet, and I could never expect anyone to understand me. Not ever. Not in a million years. I realized then, in the back of the six-by-six,

147

that if I ever wanted to be part of society again, I had to obliterate the Hotel Tacloban completely from my mind. I knew if I ever wanted to get well—if I ever wanted to be whole and normal—that I'd have to start forgetting then and there.

To tell the truth, I wouldn't have cared if no one ever did understand me or what I'd gone through, just as long as they left me alone, in peace, to recover. I wouldn't have complained or demanded special attention or special recognition; I just wanted to go home and forget the whole damn thing. I felt I deserved that much.

Just about the time we were skirting Tacloban, General Douglas MacArthur was wading ashore at Red Beach, ten miles away southeast. (Legend has it that he never even got his feet wet—that he walked *on* the water.) A little while later he would stand gallantly on the white coral sand and announce with dramatic flair, "I have returned!"

"Better Leyte then never," I say.

When I think back on it, I'm stung by the irony of his having followed me so far; me, an insignificant enlisted man. I'd left New Guinea a few short days before his arrival, and now, today, it seems like he fought the whole goddamned war on my behalf, just to rescue *me*. I know there's no logical connection, but it nevertheless seems strangely coincidental—almost predestined—and I wonder now if MacArthur knew about the Hotel Tacloban and its intrigues, or if it figured in his plans.

I was delivered in good order to a 1st Cavalry field hospital tent overlooking Cataisan airstrip, near the tiny hamlet of Burayan. The atmosphere there was friendly and relaxed, ground casualties having been lighter than expected, but a fierce air and sea battle—the historic Battle of Leyte Gulf—was just getting underway. It would persist uninterrupted for a week, and at its conclusion the Japanese Air Force and Navy would both be in ruins.

From my cot in the hospital tent I could see LSTs, PT boats, transports, Liberty ships and hospital ships ringed by warships anchored in the harbor. It was a madhouse, a logistical nightmare of epic proportions in which more than 100,000 troops and over 200,000 tons of supplies and equipment would be brought ashore in the seven days I was there.

At night I watched P-38s zoom in from the sea and land between hand-held flares on the bomb-cratered airstrip. I was very impressed by the fliers' skill and courage—the sandy runway started less than fifty feet from the shoreline—and it was amazing to me that they could distinguish between land and water. One of the orderlies explained to me that the fliers were all "hot-doggers," and that one flier in particular (a Major Bonnar or something like that) had achieved a great deal of notoriety from the press for his derring-do. Ironically, as so often happens in the heat of battle, this brave Major was accidentally shot out of the sky a few days later by an American antiaircraft crew which mistook him for a kamikaze.

I was too weak to stand by myself, and my stomach couldn't hold down solid food, so I spent my first week of freedom subsisting on soda crackers soaked in bouillon soup, resting and relaxing in the hospital tent while arrangements for my evacuation were being made. However, I had a very hard time re-orienting myself and re-establishing my identity, and at times I felt like I was coming out from under anesthesia. But the captain in charge of the field hospital and the medical personnel under his command showered me with affection and attention, and with each passing day I grew happier and more relieved. Even my distress at having been isolated from my Australian comrades began to fade, for I felt certain that they too were getting help, possibly aboard one of the hospital ships I could see anchored in the Harbor, and that seemed to be the most important thing. Even more important than my being with them.

It seemed like everyone in the US Army wanted to do little things for me; I had a pile of candy bars and gifts, and more cigarettes than I'd seen in the past two years—they came to me faster than I could smoke them. As the first POW the Americans had seen, I was the focal point of the hospital (a curiosity, I suppose, more than anything else), and until the captain sealed me off, I was visited night and day by a steady stream of well-wishers and interested medical personnel.

My most memorable visitor was a Filipino deacon from Tacloban who felt terribly bad about what had happened to me. Out of kindness, or perhaps guilt, he explained to me that Filipinos, as ardent Catholics, had formed a indivisible moral bond with the Christian west which superseded all cultural and racial ties they had with the Japanese, from whom he wished to disassociate himself completely. According to him it was only natural, after 350 years of Spanish and then 44 years of American rule, that he and his fellow Filipinos would overwhelmingly reject the Japanese in favor of the Americans, whom he welcomed as saviors. His Christian faith, he said, had given him hope, and he always knew the Yanks would come to the rescue. Just like in the movies.

Having gotten that off his chest, he picked up his mandolin and began to serenade me with a beautiful song I'll never forget, called "You Belong To My Heart." I guess it was his way to saying thanks:

You belong to my heart, now and forever,
And our love had its start, not long ago;
We were gathering stars while a million
    guitars played our love song;
When I said "I love you" every beat of
    my heart said it too.

T'was a moment like this; do you remember?
And your eyes threw a kiss, when they met mine;
Now we have all the stars and a million
    guitars are still playing:
Darling, you are the song and you'll always
    belong to my heart. *

* "You Belong To My Heart" ("Solamente Una Vez"); English words by Ray Gilbert, Spanish words by Augustan Lara; *Promotora Hispano Americana de Musica*; S.A., Mexico City, Mexico; 1941-1943/Peer International Corp.

The big moment came six or seven days after I'd been rescued, when the airstrip had been improved and transport planes could land in relative safety. All the medics from the field hospital turned out for a little bon voyage party, at which I was treated like a bona fide hero; they accompanied me to the plane (a converted C-47), patting me on the shoulder, speaking words of encouragement and wishing me well. I'd never been on an airplane before, and I was very excited, but best of all, there were female nurses waiting on board. (Army regulations wouldn't allow female nurses within a certain distance of a combat zone.) It was an exhilarating feeling being in the company of women. Man, did I feel great. I watched those disgusting Philippine Islands sink into the sea, and soon I was soaring with the clouds.

Chapter Eighteen

The C-47 made just one quick stop for refueling (I can't remember where) on the flight from Tacloban to Brisbane, Australia where I was taken to a US Naval hospital and put on a ward with seriously wounded Marines. Everywhere I looked I saw bandages and plaster casts, and everyone kept pretty much to themselves, and in many ways, especially at night, it reminded me of the Hotel Tacloban. But I was the only POW there, and I may have had the distinction of being the first American POW freed from the Philippines, not that it matters.

I stood five feet, ten inches tall and weighted 155 pounds when I lied about my age and enlisted in the US Army in the spring of 1942. When I arrived at the Navy hospital in Brisbane two and half years later, I weighed 104 pounds, *but*, remarkably, I'd grown two inches taller. My condition was listed as critical and my ailments included malaria, dysentery, yellow jaundice, beriberi, and assorted aches and pains. Nevertheless, I felt luckier than most of the men on my ward, few of whom would ever be whole. Although I stayed hooked-up to an IV for about a week, my diet soon included oatmeal, jello, and soft-boiled eggs, and I was confident of achieving a full recovery.

However, as events will soon bring to light, the US Army (which was about to come down on me hard) was aiming for something substantially less; their goal was to get me to a point where I could function minimally, to their satisfaction, but not beyond. Thanks to their guerrilla agents operating on Leyte, they'd known all along that a mutiny had occurred at the Hotel Tacloban, and they were madder than hell. From the moment I'd been separated from the Aussies on the day of our "liberation," the Army's one intention had been to keep me off-balance. My debriefing was about to begin and they didn't want me strong enough to resist.

The first inkling I had that I was in trouble came, after a grace period of about a week, when I was visited by an officer from the Judge Advocate's Office, an Irish-American from Boston with short-cropped red hair and an annoying nasal accent, who introduced himself as Captain McGrath, but who neglected to tell me why, specifically, he was there. Instead, this fellow McGrath began the debriefing by asking me if I'd like to talk about my experiences in the POW camp. My first reaction was to wonder, "Why aren't they waiting until I'm well, until I've gotten my head screwed on right?" But when it became clear during the questioning that McGrath had absolutely no interest in the circumstances of my capture, or of the events in New Guinea immediately preceeding it (which were the logical points to begin), I began to suspect that he had ulterior motives. I knew right away that I couldn't trust him and I decided *not* to offer up any information until I knew exactly what he was after.

During the hour that McGrath interrogated me that first day, he treated me, to put it bluntly, like a piece of shit—only more so than you'd ordinarily expect from an officer. In fact, when I resisted his questioning, McGrath got so upset and so abusive that one of the nurses, Mary Johnston (whom I'd had a crush on from the moment I first saw her), finally interceded on my behalf.

"Can't you see the boy's had enough for one day?" she exclaimed. That's why I liked Mary—she was caring, but she was bold, and she knew I was a wreck with no stamina at all.

But none of that mattered to McGrath—Mary was a mere lieutenant, and even though she was responsible for my well-being, she didn't have the authority to tell a captain what to do. He let her know it, too, in no uncertain terms.

"Mind your own business, nurse," he snapped at her, loud enough to let everyone on the ward know that I was bad news. "Just stay out of this, if you know what's good for you," he added menacingly.

As Mary backed off, McGrath rose from his chair, gathered his notes, looked down at me with utter contempt and said, "I'll see you tomorrow. And you'd better be more coopertive then, if *you* know what's good for you."

There were butterflies in my stomach when he left.

My comrades and I at the Hotel Tacloban had discussed how our problems with officers (and how we'd handled those problems) might affect us after our release, and we were well aware that there might be complications. But we felt sure, once the circumstances had been revealed, that everything would be foregiven. I sincerely believed that I'd acted righteously, that I had nothing to fear from my country, and that I'd be completely exonerated.

After meeting Captain McGrath, I wasn't quite so sure anymore. I'd never really known *what* to expect from the Army, but I could tell from McGrath's total indifference to both my recent ordeal and my present disability, that the one thing I shouldn't expect was sympathy. On the contrary, it appeared that a guilty verdict had already been handed down and that I was about to be served up on a platter. Although McGrath had avoided asking any direct questions about the murder, I sensed that he was leading up to it, and I had a feeling that he wanted me to spare him the trouble of a lengthy investigation by volunteering a full confession. I also had an uneasy feeling that, if he couldn't convince me to come clean, he'd settle for nothing less than my complete physical, emotional, and mental destruction. He seemed like that kind of an officer—totally turned off to humanity, a machine.

It made me mad, very mad, the more I thought about it, to think that my health and safety were still in doubt, even though I was an American POW recuperating in an American military hospital. I'd badly underestimated the forces at work behind the scenes, just as I'd underestimated the extent to which my past actions, whether justified or not, had threatened those forces. Gradually, though, I began to see that there's no escaping the military caste system, that it pokes its bloody fingers into each and every crevice in the chain of command, especially military hospitals.

Orderlies came to my cot that night, bundled me into a wheelchair, then pushed me down the hall into a room where they were showing the Bud Abbott and Lou Costello movie, "Buck Privates." In it, Bud and Lou were being inducted into

154

the Army, and Lou was having a hard time adjusting, all of which I found very funny, not having seen a movie in over two years. However, about halfway through the film I began to get sick and I passed out a few minutes later from the first malaria attack I'd had since the rescue. When I came to, back in my cot, I was completely disoriented, with no idea of where I was or why I was there. The smell of medicine and the feel of crisp, clean sheets on my body puzzled me—I thought I must be dreaming, that I'd suddenly wake up in the sick hut. I couldn't recognize my surroundings, and I thought I'd lost my mind.

As usual, the seizure subsided after about forty-eight hours and gradually I became lucid again. but from that point on I lived in perpetual dread of relapses and the terrifying nightmares and hallucinations that accompanied them—relapses which would occur regularly at bi-weekly intervals for the next few months. Indeed, malaria would drive me crazy for years to come, and not even massive doses of atabrine and quinine could reduce, let alone cure, the problem. Only when my family physician back home in Pleasantville, Dr. Hunter, began treating me after the war would I start to understand the true nature of the disease, and of its causal relationship with despondency and mental confusion. Only after Dr. Hunter had explained that to me would I stop thinking that I was insane.

I certainly had no way of learning the truth in that military hospital in Brisbane; the doctors knew, of course, but they'd been instructed not to comfort me with facts, or to explain to me that my depression and confusion were linked to my illness. The military wasn't quite sure what my status was or wasn't going to be, so, until a decision could be reached, they were content to let me hang in limbo. Throughtout the debriefing, and afterwards, too, malaria would remain the Army's principal means of keeping me off-balance.

While I was recovering from that first malaria attack, McGrath came to see me again, only this time he came equipped with a scribe who never uttered a word, but just sat there like a robot taking notes. That made me nervous. Although McGrath began the second interview by asking apparently harmless questions like: "How did the Japanese treat you?" "How much food did you receive?" "Did you receive adequate medical attention?" I knew that he was recording our conversation with the intention of using it against me. I wasn't the smartest soldier in the world, but I was smart enough to know I'd better choose my words carefully.

"What about sanitary conditions?" he asked. "Did you have soap?"

"No, nothing like that," I said.

"Were you allowed any forms of exercise?"

"No. When we weren't working, we were laying around."

"Were you allowed to communicate freely with one another?"

"At times, I guess. I don't really known what you mean."

"Forget about that for now. We'll come back to that later. Tell me, did you receive any Red Cross Packages?"

"No, never."

And on and on it went, one stupid question after another, until I grew tired of remembering, at which point McGrath (who'd noticed my yawns) started coming at me from left field, trying to trip me up.

"Were you allowed to hold religious services?"

"What do you mean?" I said, wondering what he was driving at. "I don't remember any."

"What about Easter? Were you allowed to hold religious services at Easter?"

"No. I don't remember any at Easter."

"Were you allowed to have religious services on Christmas?"

"Yeah...uh, no; I mean, I can't remember."

And then, just when I was starting to panic, he popped the sixty-four thousand dollar question: "What was the name of the ranking POW officer when you arrived in camp?"

"I don't remember," I blurted. I was exhausted and defensive and I wasn't feeling up to the kind of rigorous interogation I was getting. I knew I was backing myself into a corner, but I was only nineteen, I was sick, and I was up against a trained attorney without benefit of counsel of my own. So I decided to play dumb.

"Do you know who Major Cumyns was?"

"No. I don't know anybody by that name."

"Why wasn't he there when you were released?"

"I don't know what you're talking about."

"How did he die?"

"I just don't know," I said emphatically. "Why don't you just leave me alone and let me get well?"

I was starting to get mad, but I can also remember saying to myself, "You've got to stay cool, Doug, and not only *not* answer the questions they might think you're resisting, but also *not* answer the questions they know are harmless." I reminded myself that I wasn't merely a question of protecting myself—when I put things in perspective, I knew that my first responsibility was to the men who'd been in the POW camp with me. I knew that keeping faith with them came before obeying orders or cooperating with those who were out to entrap us. I felt I had no responsibility to anyone but to my comrades and to myself, in that order, and that everybody else, especially that asshole McGrath, could go fuck themselves. Once I'd straightened all of that out in my mind, I knew I could go resisting.

Nevertheless I was intimidated, as day after day McGrath badgered me with the same series of stupid questions while his scribe mutely took notes, compared my responses with those of previous sessions, and tugged on McGrath's sleeves whenever I contradicted myself, which was often. And when I did, McGrath would say something to the effect of, "Now, the last time I asked you this question, you said you couldn't remember, and the time before that you said, "Yes." At which point he'd lean back in his chair and fold his arms complacently across his chest. "And now you say, 'No.' " Then he'd lean forward quickly, trying to look tough, and shoot at me, "How can it be, I'd like to know, that you were able to tell us two days ago, but you can't tell us now?"

McGrath had his act down pat, and it didn't matter that he was an asshole—trained professionals like him can really put you away. He was certainly doing a number on me. "Cooperate," he was suggesting, "and we'll leave you alone. Inform on your friends and we'll let you get well."

Well, to my way of thinking, what he was offering was totally unacceptable. It was underhanded, it was demeaning, and it just wasn't right. I couldn't believe it. I couldn't believe the US Army was treating me this way, after what I'd been through on its account, and I kicked myself in the ass for ever having thought it was an institution to look up to. What a fool I'd been. All my life I'd believed that America was a force for good, and that the US Army was its one true defender. All the time I was in that godforsaken POW camp, I had put my faith in the promise that the American flag and the American people were going to protect me. The thing that hurt the most, and the question I kept asking myself, was, "Why won't they *at least* let me get well first, then let me have it?" I was tired and confused and I didn't like being pushed around, not one damn bit.

Two weeks after McGrath began his visits, around the middle of November, a second branch of the Army, G-2, sent some officers over to question me about the circumstances of my capture, starting with the events immediately preceeding it, up to and including how I was transported to Leyte and all the details in between. But G-2 wasn't as interested in hearing my story as they were in shaping it to suit their purposes, and when I recounted how the Japanese had mutilated the other men on patrol, I was accused of being a liar. Furthermore, I was warned that if I ever told anyone that story, that the US Army would say that I was deranged as a result of cerebral malaria, and they vowed they'd use that to discredit me.

I was devasted. In a way, I could understand why they wouldn't want a story like that getting out to the public; what with the war still being fought, they didn't want to scare off young recruits, of course. What I couldn't accept was their blackmailing me with malaria. Day after day they came to me, threatening me, coercing me, doing everything they could to bully me into changing my story. But I wasn't about to give in to them, either. I wasn't about to dishonor the memory of those unfortunate men on patrol by denying what had happened to them. Never. If it meant me against the US

Army, if that's what it all boiled down to, well then, that's just the way it would have to be.

By refusing to inform, I had opened myself up a barrage of psychological abuse. Pounded from the left by McGrath, hammered on the right by G-2, the cumulative pressures weighing on me at that particular time were as great as anything I'd undergone at the Hotel Tacloban. I was having malaria attacks every few days, which left me in a constant state of confusion, and I was physically wasted and showing no signs of recovering. The constant harassment, the brutal probing into my past, the character assasination, the denials, the threats, the repeated accusations that I was a liar, or worse, that I was traitor, were slowly but surely becoming too much for me to bear. The US Army was trying to wear me down, no doubt about that, and at times it seemed they were trying to finish the job the Japanese and the Major had begun. I was having an increasingly difficult time resisting the debriefing, and I kept pleading with them to let me get well, but they wouldn't let me. They wanted to break me first.

One of the tactics the Army used in its psychological war against me was isolation. Over the course of four weeks of intensive interrogation, I'd notice a radical change in attitude on the part of the nurses (except Mary) and orderlies on my ward. At first they'd been there when I needed them, but now, all of a sudden they were acting like I had some kind of terrible communicable disease—like I'd been sitting on Tojo's lap for the past two-and-a-half years—and that rankled me. The orderlies, the nurses, even the other patients looked at me, saw that I was in trouble with the authorities, and thought to themselves, "If he's in trouble and I am associated with him, or even smile at him, why then I'm liable to get into hot water, too!"

But that's where the Army made its biggest mistake. They only *assumed* that isolation would bring me to my knees. What they failed to take into consideration was that if I'd had the mental toughness to endure over two years at the Hotel Tacloban without falling to pieces, then they couldn't break me either. I'd become somewhat immune to isolation and

159

persecution, and I was quite prepared for the U.S. Army's variation on these themes. Granted the US Army employed a more sophisticated technique than the Enforcer. Sure, they confused me and made me uncertain as to where I stood within the system. And they were successful at instilling in me a profound anxiety which has lasted longer, hurt more deeply, and caused more irreparable damage to my psyche than anything I suffered in the POW camp. But they couldn't break my spirit, and that, in the final analysis, is what mattered most.

If you back a man into a corner, eventually he'll lash out, you can count on that. I did, in the only way I knew how. From the start, as was my nature, I'd had a tendency to forget the finer points of military courtesy when addressing McGrath and the officers from G-2, much to their dismay. Anyway, what began innocently enough on my part, soon developed into a game of one-upsmanship. After awhile, forgetfulness wasn't the reason why I avoided saying, "Yes, sir," and "No, sir," and all that other militaristic nonsense. And that's when the ice began to crack.

For instance, each time I requested permission to speak with Duff (a tactic I resorted to whenever I ran into a messy situation), I was reprimanded for not referring to him properly.

"Why," McGrath would ask impatiently, "are you calling him 'Duff?' His name is Lieutenant Duffy!"

"Well, you see," I'd say, satirically batting an eye, "Australian officers are a hell of a lot more relaxed than American officers."

"What do you mean by that?"

"In order to understand that, you'd first have to have some idea what it was like in a POW camp."

"How so? What haven't you told me?"

"Things there were very loose and informal. Yor know how it is, everyone was on a first name basis."

"You're making it sound like a goddamned resort."

"Yeah. That's it! Now you got the picture."

But my insolence played right into their hands, of course, and they used that against me, too. They said I was undisciplined, insubordinate, and they said that I lacked respect for authority. In short, they were building a military case against me.

Chapter Nineteen

Captain McGrath and an officer from G-2 came to see me sometime in mid-December, 1944, only this time McGrath came right out with it and said that all I'd been doing was telling them lies. He was paticularly upset at me for claiming not to remember the Major. McGrath asked me point blank, "How could Major Cumyns be the ranking POW officer for over a year, and you not know who he was?"

Although it seemed funny at the time, I realize now that denying any knowledge of the Major was my biggest mistake; my only excuse is that, being young and naive, I really didn't know what else to say.

McGrath hit the ceiling. "You're lying, damn you, and you'd better stop it fast," he screamed at me. Only when he said "fast" it came out sounding like "fost," and I couldn't help snickering at his accent.

"You might not think this is so goddamned funny for long," he hissed. "You're heading straight for a preliminary court-martial review board, you know."

I'd suspected all along that he was working up to something like that, although I must admit I had no idea what a preliminary court-martial review board was. But, whatever it was, it wasn't good—I knew that much. I felt those old familiar fingers clutching at my throat, warning me that I was skating on very thin ice.

"You'll be spending the next twenty-five years in a military stockade, if you're lucky," McGrath said venomously. "I hope you enjoy yourself. You seem to like being in prison." Then he went on to say that I was a disgrace to the United States Army and to the American people for what I'd done, and on and on.

But I didn't give a damn. I was determined not to implicate my comrades. I was determined to keep the soldier's faith no matter what the consequences were.

Just prior to Christmas, two hulking military policemen swaggered onto my ward without warning, collected me and escorted me to a sparsely furnished room down the hall. Why they felt they needed MPs I'm not quite sure, though I suppose they felt I might try to go over the wall. Anyway, the three of us marched into the room in single file, with me in the middle, then the MPs fanned out on either side of me and came to a snappy salute. I, on the other hand, made it a point to keep my hands in the pockets of my hospital gown, and I stood at ease. Before me, three men sat at a long wooden table, otherwise the room was bare. My eyesight still wasn't up to par, and it was hard for me to distinguish between gold oak leaf, silver oak leaf, and silver eagle, but I could plainly see that the three officers seated at the tribunal (a major, a lieutenant colonel and a full colonel, I believe) were deeply insulted by what I'd done. They were all regular army, all older men who gave no names, all angry men who just sat there glowering.

To my surprise the MPs left the room, leaving the four of us alone. No scribes were present to record what was said, and the officers didn't even bother questioning me; rather, the Major began by informing me that they already had all the pertinent facts, that they'd had them all along, and they did. They had "The Book" in their possession as well as signed statements from all the British soldiers detailing precisely what had transpired at the Hotel Tacloban. They told me the whole story, including the roles Donaldson, Courtney and I had played in the Major's assasination. They told me that I was in deep trouble and that I could be executed for that I had done. They said there was a chance that might happen, but they wanted to hear my side of the story first.

That was the first time anybody had asked to hear my version, and I jumped at the chance. I talked to them for over an hour, until I grew so tired of talking that they called in an MP to fetch a chair so I could finish my story sitting down. I talked and I talked and I told them the whole sordid tale, form beginning to end. And while I was spilling my guts, I sensed peripherally that one of the officers directing questions at me (I think it was the full colonel) seemed a trifle sympathetic. Maybe he'd seen combat, or had a son in the war, or maybe he just felt sorry for me; in any event, he seemed genuinely moved by my description of the hardships we suffered, and at times he smiled reassuringly with his crinkled eyes. There was a sense of communication between us, a bond, so I directed my answers back to him, regardless of who had asked the question. I felt I had a friend, or at least someone who was willing to listen, so I talked and talked until finally I became so exhausted that they dismissed me, and I returned to my ward and collapsed on my cot.

A period of more than a week went by, during which time Mary and I celebrated Christmas together on my ward, because the US Army wouldn't allow me to leave the hospital to spend the holiday on her family's sheep farm just outside Brisbane. I'd liked Mary from the moment I first saw her, and over time, out of compassion and later respect, she'd grown to like me. She was bright and scrubbed clean, tall and slim and shapely—an undaunted, uninhibited woman several years older than I who I'll always remember dressed in her sexy white nurse's outfit, her dark hair cut in a pageboy, her wide mouth smiling lustily, optimistically. With Mary's help, I began to find happiness in the world once again. Like Bobby and Duffy before her, Mary was there for me to lean on at a critical time in my life, and I couldn't have made it without her. She gave me hope.

And hope was about all I had then—I heard absolutely nothing concerning my status from the military tribunal over the Christmas vacation, and the suspense was nerve-racking. There was little for me to do, other than to reflect on what had already happened, or else to speculate on what might happen next. And yet somewhere in the back of my mind I knew that everything was going to turn out all right. You can chalk it up to Mary, or that kindly old colonel, or to some irrational teenage faith in the existence of a morally ordered universe (a benign God?). Or maybe I'm just a hopeless romantic. Whatever the reason or reasons, I was sure I had "rights." I naturally assumed that, as a American citizen and soldier, when the going got tough, I could at least speak to someone (a lawyer, perhaps) who was qualified to instruct me in any rights I did have coming to me.

But I was wrong. Like every other military organization in the world (all of which, at the highest level, are one and the same), the US Army is structured on the chain of command, and without it, it ceases to exist. Therefore, to the extent which my crime had deserated that sacred order, I had automatically abrogated my rights within the military infrastructure. The fact of the matter is this: the U.S. Army is a predatory beast with the capability to destroy anything that threatens it, from within or without. It recognizes no authority above itself, and within itself it need offer no justice, no justification, no mercy.

Realizing that gave me an awesome, helpless feeling.

A few days after Christmas, the same two MPs returned to my ward and carted me back to the same room where the same three officers were waiting. Once again the MPs left us alone in the room, and once again I noticed that no one was recording what I said or what was said to me—and I took that to be a sign that things were going my way. It just seemed to me, in this childish, uneducated mind of mine, that if they were seriously building a case against me, then at this point they would be writing everything down. Of course there would never be any transcripts from my hearing before the preliminary kangaroo court-martial review board, just as there would never be any documentation of the Hotel Tacloban. The outcome had been fixed from the start; up until now it had all been a cruel charade, a show of force intended to frighten and confuse me—to make me grab at the "compromise" solution they had concocted to protect themselves, not me.

The full colonel, the man I felt was my sponsor, began by telling me that, according to statements given to the review board by my Australian comrades, my day-to-day conduct in the POW camp had been exemplary. In fact the Australians, God bless 'em, had recommended that I be awarded the Distinguished Service Cross for conspicuous gallantry. Only the Medal of Honor is higher. But, the colonel continued, they couldn't give it to me because that would be the same thing as admitting that the Hotel Tacloban had existed, and they couldn't possibly do *that*. Instead, for my own good, as well as for the good of the military service, they'd arranged a cover-up in which all records of my service in New Guinea and the POW camp were to be changed. I was to be given a new serial number, a new date of induction, a new, fictitious record of service in the 375th Harbor Craft Company, a new medical history, and, most importantly, an honorable discharge. In addition, all evidence of the Hotel Tacloban and the unfortunate events which occurred there was to be destroyed, and the US Army would forever deny that anything other than what appeared on my new papers was true. That was a promise.

The colonel went on to explain that they were doing me this favor in as much as I was so very young and probably could not have exerted any influence over the plans which were made and carried out, and in view of my otherwise exemplary behavior. However, he emphasized, the killing of an officer who was merely conducting his duty in the manner he felt best, constituted an outrageous violation of all miltary rules and traditions, and therefore, before I was let off the hook, I must first agree *never*, repeat *never* to contact *any* of the Australians who were with me in camp. That was the deal. It was explained to me unequivocably that this was for the good of my comrades, who as older men, and, whether they liked it or not, as members of the English military, were being held fully accountable for the crime.

The message they sent me was loud and clear; if I ever uttered one word about the Hotel Tacloban to anyone, my comrades would suffer. It was not, as the saying goes, an offer I could easily refuse, so very reluctantly I agreed to their terms. But in one sense I felt I'd won a small victory. In holding out for a long as I did, I'd made them realize that my personality wasn't constructed along military lines, and that if they wanted to secure my cooperation, they'd have to appeal to me on a more human level. In getting them to back off, I'd forced them to do a very unnatural thing, and that gave me a sense of satisfaction. What's more, I was proud of the way I'd conducted myself, and I was proud to learn that the Aussies, for whom I had so much love and respect, felt I was a good enough soldier to deserve recognition in the form of a DSC. Not getting it was a bit of a disappointment, but what the hell, I can live without it.

I was relieved, to say the very least, and I returned to my cot pretending they really had done me a favor. Because I'd been listed as Missing In Action (MIA), they could have locked me away forever, and no one ever would have known; that's what I told myself, even though deep down inside I knew I'd been railroaded—that the army was merely protecting itself from embarrassment. I knew I was a victim of irregular procedures, that I'd never been arrested or charged, and that even military law prohibits compulsory self-incrimination. I knew that if I'd had a halfway decent attorney, I could have exposed them for the assholes they truly were. But the knowledge that I was getting out at long last, relatively intact and with an honorable discharge, greatly overshadowed all other considerations. I just hoped that I could recover my health, pick up the broken pieces of my life, and proceed from there. I was perfectly willing to forget the whole damn thing.

They kept me in the hospital for another six weeks, until I weighed close to 120 pounds, because the war was still being fought and they didn't want people (especially new troops on the docks waiting to go overseas) to see the US Army unloading a soldier in my condition. That would have been bad for morale, and I'm sure they wanted to fatten me up before they placed me on the altar.

Except for Mary (who took me home with her one weekend and put my worst fears about my manhood to rest), no one spoke to me during those last six weeks, other than to say, "Roll over, we're going to give you a shot," and, "Get your gear together, you're going home." I was roundly shunned but I really didn't care anymore. I was intelligent enough to know that if I told anyone what I've just told you, the person would have said, "This guy's sick! Where'd he come up with a cockamamie story like that?"

MacArthur had landed on Luzon and retaken Manila. Superfortress bombers based in the Philippines were destroying Japanese cities, and the US Marines were storming ashore on Iwo Jima when they sent me home in February, 1945. They sent me home on a troopship, not a hospital ship, because my medical records had been doctored and now read, "No Malaria, No Dysentery." Incidentally, it had taken over a month coming over, and I was pleasantly surprised when the voyage back home took only twelve days.

It was very exciting being back in the states, what with all the fanfare and everything, and the first thing they did when we disembarked at Fort Ord was to take us to the mess for a steak dinner with mashed potatoes and string beans and all the trimmings. But my stomach couldn't digest the meat (which had been over-cooked, anyway), and I passed out from a malaria attack during the meal. There followed a great deal of confusion concerning my inexplicable medical condition—my records indicated quite clearly "No Malaria, No Dysentery," and no one doubted them for a minute, but there I was having fever and chills, and that was hard to explain. I tried to tell them, but they refused to pay any attention, and I was sent to the laboratory for a blood test, where I subsequently passed out cold before they could extract a sample. That gave them just the excuse they needed—the orderlies said I was afraid of needles, that's all, then they laughed at me and called me a sissy.

I spent the next two weeks in a military hospital at Fort Ord, lost in a tangle of red tape, begging the doctors to let me go home, and eventually they handed me a government meal ticket and loaded me on a civilian train bound for Penn Station. They were glad to get me out of their hair, but things didn't get any better for me; about the time we reached Reno, Nevada, I had another malaria attack which I rode out on the train with the help of a married couple sitting opposite me (they had a son in the service) who brought me soup during the stops. At one point the wife collared an MP and asked him to help me out, but when he read my papers and saw they were stamped, "No Malaria, No Dysentry," he became very upset and accused me of drinking. I began to see the writing on the wall.

When the train pulled into jam-packed Penn station, I was simply amazed at the throng of happy-go-lucky people waiting on ticket lines. There were more of them (especially soldiers and sailors) moving back and forth across the country than the public transportation system could handle, and the place was literally overflowing. And of course everything was being done according to "priority," with servicemen having "priority" over civilians, and officers in ascending rank having "priority" over enlisted men. But no one seemed to mind the discrimination—people were going back to work in droves, finally, and the entire nation was vibrating from a sense of urgency and collective purpose. This was the way I remembered it—upbeat, alive, vigorous; couples embracing and passionately kissing goodbye; engineers blowing their whistles and conductors yelling, "All Abroad!;" distraught wives and fiancées cloaked in clouds of locomotive steam, weeping and waving white handkerchiefs farewell. I felt a sudden twinge of sadness knowing that no sweetheart was waiting for me. But at least I'd made it home, goddammit, and I felt pretty good about that.

I stood around and watched for awhile—watched and listened and tasted and smelled—letting the flood of sensations wash away my memories. But I had a hard time shaking off the irony of so many grateful people offering their seats to men in uniform—boys, really—hustling off to meet unhappy, abbreviated fates. I knew it would be hard to forget.

And there was still one fight left. I'd made it through the POW camp, and I'd made it through the debriefing—the only thing left was to get them to change my papers. I didn't want to spend the rest of my life passing out on trains, or in my dessert, and having no one believe I was sick because my papers said I wasn't. "Papers!" The last, the greatest enemy of them all. Ready for a fight, I boarded a bus bound for Camp Upton, New Jersey, where I was scheduled to received my mustering out papers, and when I got there I argued with the clerk over the false information, and at first I refused to sign unless he erased the "No Malaria, No Dysentry" stamp. But he wouldn't change the papers, of course; "Not on your life, buddy," the staff Sergeant said. And once I got there and saw the end in sight, I just couldn't wait to get it over with—eagerness to be done with the whole thing got the best of me, and I signed. It was exhilarating, but I shouldn't have done it. But I did, and they gave me my ruptured duck, and that was the end of my military career. From Camp Upton I took a bus to Grand Central station and from there I rode a train home to Pleasantville. Home at last.

Epilogue

In retrospect, I don't think that I amount to any more or less than anyone else because of what happened to me—not by any stretch of the imagination. Like the holocaust victims and Vietnam veterans I empathize so closely with, I just happened to be in the particular time and place—that's all. The only thing my experience makes me is a survivor.

When I got home, the world seemed pretty and small and I was disappointed to find that all the same prejudices were still in vogue; but it was peaceful, and that was enough to make me happy. I got a job driving a truck for Railway Express, and I kept to myself.

I wrote a letter to Charley Ferguson almost immediately. It came back stamped "Deceased."

I learned that my mother had been visited by representatives of the US Army a few weeks before my arrival, while I was still listed as MIA, and that, on their request, she'd sent all my military records to Washington, DC. They all came back changed.

Eight years after my discharge, in 1953, I was still having frequent malaria attacks, so I called the Veterans Administration for help. They told me that it was impossible for the strain of malaria I claimed to have to be active after five years, and they said I was lying. Dr. Hunter was treating me at the time, and of course he knew I had malaria, but there was nothing he could do to change the Army's mind and he advised me to forget about it. But the attacks persisted until finally I collapsed at work and was taken to Northern Westchester Hosptial. On October 8, 1955, blood smears taken while my fever was raging contained the malaria parasite. It's on the record.

My older brother Ed, who was seriously wounded at Saint Lo in France when his tank took a direct hit from a German artillery shell, stayed in the Army and advanced to the rank of Lieutenant-Colonel. For awhile he served in Germany during the occupation, and later he was stationed at the Pentagon, where he had several high level contacts, but when I asked him to help straighten out my medical records so I could get some financial aid, he refused. He was in complete sympathy with the Army. Unlike me, he has a military mind; his kids called him "sir" and stand at attention when he enters the room. I never trusted him enough to tell him about the Hotel Tacloban; but of course, up until now I hadn't told anybody.

You already know about my medical problems, about the heart surgery and the strokes, so it'll come as no surprise when I say that I made funeral arrangements the other day, which, coincidentally, was October 20, 1982—thirty-eight years after my "liberation." Anyway, without getting morbid, there are two parts to a funeral, one being emotional and the other being financial, and it's easier for everyone involved if the latter part is planned out ahead of time. There's absolutely nothing ghoulish about it, it just helps the survivors get through a time in their lives when they're vulnerable and easily taken advantage of by society's predators. The funeral home I've hired is located in a building which previously housed a bank, which I'm sure will please my Scottish ancestors (on my father's side of the family) immensely. The grave site is on the side of a hill in Sleepy Hollow Cemetery in Tarrytown; it's a beautiful spot and I'm satisfied to know that is where my bones will spend eternity.

One last word about eternity: I know it sounds unsophisticated, but I stopped believing in God when Bobby died. Corny as it may sound, I just couldn't understand why God would take a truly decent person while allowing evil men to go on living. It just didn't make sense. In fact, it's taken me until now to completely understand, and to learn to live with the fact, that God doesn't decide who'll live and who'll die; God doesn't kill people, people kill people.

What's frustrating is that so many deadly devices still exist to be leveled against millions of innocent people in the name of God, by leaders who use the authority of the Bible (or whatever) as justification for killing so-called inferior or immoral or God-less races. People continue to kill people, and the horrendous thing about it is that it has nothing to do with knowledge or intelligence or wisdom. People simply continue to kill people, on a grand scale.

The decision to launch World War Three will not be made democratically. It will not be the result of a national referendum and it won't reflect the majority opinion. The decision to unleash Armageddon will be made by relatively few people sitting at the top of the chain of command, and only one man acting under superior orders will push the button. To do this without remorse, this man need only *believe* that "his" way of life is under mortal attack, and that justice demands the destruction of the enemy.

Lieutenant Calley was merely following orders. The men who incinerated Hiroshima and Nagasaki were merely following orders. They did their duty and they felt no remorse. Likewise, when the President (or whoever) says, "Fire!" some good soldier somewhere will do it, because blind obedience to authority exempts him from individual moral responsibility for his actions. Unwilling to desecrate the chain of command, he will be unable to do the disobedient deed which would save the world from destruction.

I never had the capacity to descend into mindless obedience, and that failing got me into hot water with the authorities. For the past forty years I've wondered when the MPs were going to come crashing through the front door to arrest me. But now that my time—possibly the world's time—is at hand, I just don't care. Let them come. I died several times in those lousy islands, died the coward's death. But never again. No more deals. Let freedom ring!

Acknowledgment

Based primarily on his recollections, *The Hotel Tacloban* is the true account of my father's wartime experiences as an infantryman in New Guinea, as a prisoner of war in a Japanese camp on the island of Leyte in the Philippines, and as a patient in a military hospital in Brisbane, Australia. However, to provide the uninformed reader with a sense of perspective, the story has been set against an historical background. Historical and factual information was drawn from the following sources, which I would now like to thank:

Cannon, Dr. M. Hamlin: *Leyte: The Return to the Philippines* (Office of the Chief of Military History, Department of the Army, Washington, D.C.; 1954).

Lear, Elmer: *The Japanese Occupancy of the Philipines: Leyte, 1941-1945, Data Paper #42*; (Southeast Asia Program, Wagner College, Cornell University, Ithaca, New York; June, 1961.)

Mayo, Lida: *Bloody Buna* (Doubleday & Company, Inc., New York; 1974).

Milner, Samuel: *Victory in Papua* (Office of the Chief of Military History, Department of the Army, Washington, D.C.; 1957).

Reader's Digest: *The Illustrated Story of World War II* (Reader's Digest Association, Pleasantville, New York; 1969).

Smyth, John: *Sandhurst* (London, Weidenfield, 1961).

Steinberg, David Joel: *Philippines Collaboration in World War II* (University of Michigan Press, Ann Arbor; 1967).

Steinberg, Rafael: *Return to the Philippines* (Time/Life Books, Alexandria, Virginia; 1979).

U.S. Army. Forces, Pacific. General Staff. Military Intelligency Section: *Intelligence Series. Volume 1: The Guerrilla Resistance Movement in the Philippines, with appendices.* Mimeo, General Headquarters, Far East Command, Tokyo, 1948. FEC/MIS/v.1.

U.S. Army. Forces, Pacific. General Staff. Military Intelligence Section. *Intelligence Series. Volume 2. Intelligence Activities in the Philippines During the Japanese Occupancy, with appendices.* Mimeo, General Headquarters, Far East Command, Tokyo, 1948. FEC/MIS/v.2.

U.S. Army. Forces, Pacific. General Staff. Military Intelligence Section. *A*

Brief History of the G-2 Section, GHQ, SWPA and Affiliated Units: Introduction to the Intelligence Series. Mimeo, General Headquarters, Far East Command, Tokyo, 1948. FEC/MIS/Intro.

I would also like to thank the following authors for supplemental information, insights and firsthand observations on the battle for New Guinea and the POW experience:

Alibury, Alfred: *Bamboo and Bushido* (London, World Distributors; 1965).

Benson, James: *Prisoner's Base and Home* (Robert Hale, London, 1957).

Brines, Russell: *Until They Eat Stones* (J. B. Lippincott & Company, Philadelphia and New York; 1944).

Gordon, Ernest: *Through the Valley of the Kwai* (Harper and Row, New York; 1962).

Ingham, Travis: *Rendezvous by Submarine* (Doubleday, Doran & Company, Garden City; 1945).

Johnston, George: *New Guinea Diary* (Victor Gollancz Ltd., London, 1944).

Johnston, George: *The Toughest Fighting in the World* Duell, (Sloan & Pearce, New York; 1943).

Josephy, Alvin M. Jr.: *The Long and the Short and the Tall* (Alfred Knopf, New York; 1946.)

Kahn, E. J.: *GI Jungle* (Simon & Schuster, New York; 1943).

Keith, Agnes Newton: *Three Came Home* (Little Brown & Company, U.S.; 1946).

MacArthur, Douglas: *Reminiscences* (McGraw-Hill, New York, 1964.)

Paul, Raymond: *Retreat From Kokoda* (Heinemann, Melbourne, 1958).

Reading, Geoffrey: *Papuan Story* (Angus & Robertson, Australia, 1946).

Rivett, Robert D.: *Behind Bamboo* (Angus & Robertson, Australia, 1946).

Robinson, Pat: *The Fight For New Guinea* (Random House, New York, 1943).

Russel, Edward: *The Knights of Bushido* (Cassell & Company, Ltd., London; 1958).

White, Osmar: *Green Armor* (Norton, New York; 1945).

Wolfert, Ira: *An American Guerrilla in the Philippines* (Simon & Schuster, New York; 1945)